COMMUNICATE, LEAD, AND TRANSFORM

Behaviors to Break Free from Your Mental Wheel Ruts

WILLIAM J. MURRAY, PhD, PMI-ACP, PMP
EDDIE MERLA, PMI-ACP, PMP

T0350715

Library of Congress Cataloging-in-Publication Data
Names: Murray, William J., 1945– author. | Merla, Eddie, author.
Title: Communicate, lead, and transform / William J. Murray PMI-ACP, PMP,
    Eddie Merla PMI-ACP, PMP.
Description: Plantation, FL : J. Ross Publishing, [2022] | Includes bibliographical
    references and index.
Identifiers: LCCN 2022019520 (print) | LCCN 2022019521 (ebook) |
    ISBN 9781604271867 (paperback) | ISBN 9781604278439 (epub)
Subjects: LCSH: Communication in management. | Leadership. |
    BISAC: BUSINESS & ECONOMICS / Business Communication / General |
    BUSINESS & ECONOMICS / Leadership
Classification: LCC HD30.3 .M877 2022 (print) | LCC HD30.3 (ebook) |
    DDC 658.4/5—dc23/eng/20220511
LC record available at https://lccn.loc.gov/2022019520
LC ebook record available at https://lccn.loc.gov/2022019521

Phone: (954) 727-9333
Fax: (561) 892-0700
Web: www.jrosspub.com

CONTENTS

PREFACE

Numerous books on how to improve your leadership and communication skills are based solely on theory or the author's experiences. This is not one of them. This book employs an empirical approach to meaningful improvement and aims to help you leverage your own observations, experiences, and learning experiments, not just ours as the authors. You'll be asked to think about what worked and what didn't, as well as what you did to achieve or hinder your desired outcomes. You will also be asked to elaborate on what behaviors you believe you should start, increase, stop, or decrease. Throughout this book, we will share our observations and what we have learned over many decades of training leaders in order to assist you with identifying focus areas for improvement. As you might infer, the emphasis is a hands-on, practical application of behavior-based skills and how to grow into a successful communicator and, ultimately, a leader.

Leadership and its supporting skill, *communication*, impact everyone, regardless of their position or role in an organization or whether we are referring to our personal or professional lives. Consider how your communication skills have influenced your life. You can probably think of numerous instances when you were an excellent communicator and others when you were not. Consider others who have influenced your life. Was their ability to communicate a critical component of their effectiveness? Almost everyone to whom we pose this question responds, "Yes." As a result, we believe that communication is one of the most critical skills to acquire as you make your way through life and on your journey to effective leadership.

THE IMPORTANCE OF COMMUNICATION TODAY

Effective communication skills are more important than ever as we try to navigate through a world with numerous socioeconomic hurdles: the *(continues)*

COVID-19 pandemic, racial injustice, migration/immigration disruption, unending political rhetoric, and the wail of those who feel they have been left behind. Pick up a newspaper, listen to a newscast, or open your smartphone to see the preponderance of evidence telling us that we are talking louder than ever to ears that are not listening and to minds so tired that they are closed.

The skill-building information in this book is based upon the research of successful leaders and our own experiences with thousands of people during our working, consulting, and training careers. These professional experiences have taken place in some of the largest oil, petrochemical, healthcare, airline, banking, and information technology organizations in the world. Our academic experiences as adjunct professors at Rice University and the University of Houston, as well as being certified trainers for the Project Management Institute, have reinforced our conviction that good communication is a vital component of a leader's success.

So, how do leaders communicate to transform organizations? It encompasses more than just motivational lectures. A splendid illustration is the story of the transformation of Continental Airlines in the late 1990s under CEO Gordon Bethune[1] and COO Greg Brenneman.[2] Continental offered employees a $65 bonus every month that Continental was among the top five U.S. airlines with on-time arrivals. When the checks were first issued, Kay, Gordon's administrative assistant, waved her check and thanked Gordon for acknowledging everyone's work. Gordon looked at the check and said, "This is not $65." Kay responded with, "They have to take out taxes." Gordon picked up the phone, called HR, and told them to "Gross up all the checks and ensure that everyone receives $65." It cost Continental less than $10 per employee per month for this modification, but the tale spread like wildfire throughout the company. Senior executives at Continental began to listen and communicate the importance of employees by deeds, not just words. Bethune developed a strong team at Continental, fostering relationships and trust across the firm. Continental moved from being the poorest among the largest airlines in the United States to being first in all 10 of the Department of Transportation's customer service indicators in less than a year. By the way, the initiative was self-funding due to the cost savings associated with fewer flight delays and cancellations.

Transformative communication and leadership behaviors involve a commitment to improvement, patience, practice, change, hard work, and small victories in order to reinforce your efforts. However, you have to start somewhere. This book is intended to serve as a jumping-off point. We wish you success on your adventure!

ENDNOTES

1. Bethune, Gordon. 1998. *From Worst to First: Behind the Scenes of Continental's Remarkable Comeback*. New York. John Wiley & Sons, Inc.
2. Brenneman, Greg. "Right Away and All at Once: How We Saved Continental," *Harvard Business Review*, Sept–Oct 1998, pp. 162–168.

ACKNOWLEDGMENTS

Many people have contributed to the successful completion of this book. Truth be known, the success of this book is due more to the excellent staff of our publisher J. Ross Publishing and our colleagues who have reviewed many drafts of this book and provided value-added comments and suggestions. The authors take full responsibility for any shortcomings.

We would like to specifically thank:

- Stephen Buda at J. Ross Publishing for his many reviews of our work and his excellent questions and suggestions.
- Deborah McCoy for her excellent comments, especially about giving feedback.
- Jamie Ressler with his eagle eyes caught many spelling and punctuation errors as well as his suggestions on building teams and referring us to General Stanley McChrystal's excellent book *Team of Teams*.
- Andrea Lapsley provided helpful comments on our chapter roadmaps.
- Isaac Montoya provided candid comments on the opening chapters and how they helped (or hindered) the reader's journey.
- Dr. Kurt Edwards gave us a physician's perspective on our efforts and helped clarify many of the concepts presented in this book.
- Patrick Handley of the INSIGHT Institute did yeoman's work in reviewing and editing Chapter 3 in regards to the INSIGHT Inventory®. In addition, thank you, Patrick, for recommending excellent editors Kristen at Upwork and Imane at Fiverr.
- Special thanks to Kate and Jenny Murray for editing efforts early on.

Besides the list above, a big thank you goes to the students at the Glasscock School of Continuing Studies at Rice University who attended our soft school classes and validated many of the exercises contained in this book. These exercises are the bedrock for building new habits for improving communication and leadership.

Bill Murray
Eddie Merla
June 2022

ABOUT THE AUTHORS

William J. Murray has over 45 years of industry experience including senior management at a large multinational chemical company; owner and managing director of W J Murray & Associates, a strategic management consulting organization; and as a senior consulting manager at Expressworks International, LLC, a change management consulting organization. He has also served as an adjunct professor at Rice University and the University of Houston. Bill's consulting focus is on assisting leaders in the development

and, more important, the execution of strategic plans. His consulting clients have included IBM, Chevron, Shell Oil of North America, United Airlines, Exxon Mobil, Rolls Royce, BMC Software, Kellogg Brown and Root, Baylor College of Medicine, Baker Ripley House, Saudi Aramco, the University of Texas Health Science Center, and the European Academy for Thoracic and Cardiac Surgery Limited.

During Murray's career, he realized the challenge people had with changing their behaviors. To grow professionally, people must often adopt new behaviors and/or abandon behaviors that have become ingrained habits. Bill developed a passion to provide a more realistic pathway to change rather than offering people a list of *do's* and *don'ts*. This pathway involves a commitment to change, hard work, patience, persistence, and a roadmap to guide people through the process of developing more productive behaviors.

Murray earned his undergraduate degree in chemical engineering from Texas Tech University and his MBA and Ph.D. in industrial psychology from the University of Utah. Murray also holds the Project Management Professional (PMP)® and Agile Certified Practitioner (PMI-ACP)® certifications from the Project Management Institute.

Eddie Merla, PMI-ACP, PMP, is the owner and founder of Duende Project Management Services, a training and consulting company. Over his many decades of experience, Eddie has implemented project management programs, strategies, and best practices for multiple organizations and in multiple industries. His project management engagements have included North America, Europe, the Middle East, South America, and Asia. He has also implemented organizational structures to support large projects and improve the delivery of project and program results. In addition, Eddie has coached corporate clients in the transition from traditional project management practices to agile methods.

As a trainer and coach, Eddie has trained several thousand project management professionals throughout the world on project management, leadership, and soft skills topics. He has published articles with the Project Management Institute (PMI) and has been a frequent speaker at PMI Global Congresses, including the Latin America Congress, the EMEA Congress, the Asia Pacific Congress, and the North America Congress.

Eddie is an instructor at the Rice University Glasscock School of Continuing Education on project management topics, including preparing students for the Project Management Professional (PMP)® exam. Also at Rice Glasscock, he served as the primary subject matter expert for the development of the Strategic Project Management course and codeveloped the Soft Skills for Business Professionals course to help executives develop their communications and leadership skills.

If our book has helped you identify and change behaviors that has made you a more effective communicator and leader, please feel free to recommend it to others in your organization. In addition, we are available to provide seminars and workshops to take teams through a process of identifying desired communication and leadership behaviors and building habits to improve identified skill sets. To learn more about seminar and workshops offerings, contact either of the authors at:

Bill Murray—wjcm@wjmurray-assoc.com
Eddie Merla—eddiemerla@duendepm.com

CHAPTER 1

COMMUNICATE, LEAD, AND TRANSFORM

"The difference between mere management and leadership is communication."

—Winston Churchill

CHAPTER ROADMAP

This book will guide you on a journey to assess and improve your communication and leadership skills in the shortest amount of time. The skills addressed in this 14-chapter book include: disagreeing well, listening, building high performance teams, self-awareness, and relationship building—to name just a few. All topics are discussed in terms of communication and leadership. More specifically, the goals of this chapter are to:

1. Provide a definition of key terms used in this book to ensure understanding of processes, tools, and techniques presented.
2. Present the behavioral foundations for this book.
3. Provide a roadmap of how this book is organized to assist you in developing more effective communication and leadership skills (see Figure 1.1).

In addition to those three goals, this chapter also provides an overview of:

1. Part I: Communication
2. Part II: Leadership
3. Part III: Transformation—transforming skill areas you identify as crucial to improving your success as a communicator and as a leader into goals, plans to achieve those goals, and how you will measure progress

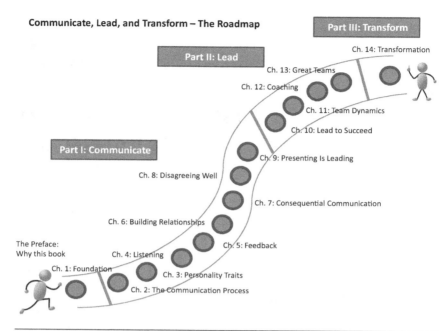

Figure 1.1   Chapter roadmap

1.1 THE DEFINITIONS

Communication, leadership, and transformation are powerful terms. As authors, we are committed and passionate about helping people become successful in all three. But skill development is a process with multiple levels of learning required to break the wheel ruts of the past and develop the skills and underlying behaviors necessary to produce success. It is important before we begin the journey of skill development to align the meaning of key terms and phrases used throughout this book:

1. **Skill:** A skill is the learned ability to do something well.[1] Skills are developed through learning, practice, and experience and enable people to perform an activity successfully. Skill is acquired after putting in a lot of hard work and using all available resources to develop it. Skills can be in technical activities such as writing software or investigating scientific questions. In this book, we will focus on *soft skills* such as communication, working well in a team, listening, leading, etc.

2. **Behavior:** A behavior is anything a person does in response to stimulation.[2] Behaviors can be thoughts, feelings, or physical

activity or all three in some sequence. It is important to clarify how skills and behaviors are related. *Listening is a skill. How a person listens is a behavior.* Let's say that a person listens (a skill) in order to respond (a behavior) so that when the speaker is finished talking, the listener is prepared with counterpoints (i.e., listening to respond). Now assume our listener (after reading Chapter 4, Listen Better to Succeed) decides to improve their listening skills by *listening to understand.* The skill is still listening but to improve it, our listener must change their behavior. Practicing new behaviors is therefore necessary for skill development. This book is focused on helping you practice behaviors that result in building skills in areas you have identified as important for you to grow as a communicator and a leader. Consequently, you will see the term *behavior-based skills* throughout this book in order to underscore the importance of the need to change behaviors in order to develop effective skills.

3. **Focus area:** *Focus area* is the term used in this book to identify higher priority behavior-based skills. There are tools, techniques, and exercises to assist you in identifying areas for development of behavior-based skills in each chapter. Among the many opportunities for development, you will be asked to prioritize those that will have the greatest impact on your abilities at the end of each chapter and to further prioritize focus areas at the conclusion of the three parts of this book.

Let's pause to confirm that we are all on the same page regarding the development of focus areas. Think of focus areas as zones of emphasis that you believe will help you improve your communication or leadership behaviors. For example, in Chapter 5 you will be asked to review your experiences in receiving and giving feedback. As a result of that review, you jot down a brief note like "provide more impactful feedback" as a focus area. Additional reading in Chapter 5 and in other chapters may help you identify additional focus areas or assist you in clarifying a previously identified focus area. For instance, further reading in Chapter 5 may prompt you to rephrase the focus area from simply "provide more impactful feedback" to something more descriptive, such as "when providing feedback to someone about performance relative to expectations, begin by having them assess their performance on ways they can improve."

1.2 THE FOUNDATION

Allow us to be candid about the nature of the journey through this book—it involves change. More precisely, this book is about helping you to change and this process requires you to identify what you wish to change (i.e., your focus areas). You will *transform* your highest priority focus areas into specific goals, build plans to help you reach your goals, and determine how you will measure progress (Chapter 14). The underlying premise is that growth involves *changing your behaviors*.

A person is usually considered a skilled communicator based on the behaviors that others observe. Consequently, you will see the term *behaviors* throughout this book. Furthermore, when behaviors are continually practiced, they become habits. These habits (i.e., mental wheel ruts) may be productive and others far less so. Ray Dalio's advice was on point when he said, "Choose your habits carefully because they are one of the most powerful tools in your brain's toolbox."[3]

Why are habits hard to change? Research on the brain shows that people enhance their neural networks when they continually practice behaviors.[4] Your brain changes (neural scientists call this concept *neuroplasticity*).[5] These repeatedly exercised behaviors strengthen neural networks and become wheel ruts in our brains, causing us to become stuck in either good or bad habits. As an analogy, consider the concept of muscle memory. Golfers such as Tiger Woods, gymnasts such as Simone Biles, and tennis players such as Novak Djokovic have spent nearly every day, week, month, and year practicing. They strengthen particular neural networks. When Tiger Woods approaches a golf ball, he is not thinking about how to move his club through the swing. His muscle memory takes over in the form of a habit.

POWER OF EFFECTIVE HABITS

Doing something well—simply out of habit—was displayed by Breanna Stewart, one of the stars of the U.S. women's basketball team that won the gold medal at the Tokyo Olympics in 2021. She showed the capacity for basketball excellence without the need for complex calculations. "To be honest," Stewart said about how her mind works during one of her basketball masterpieces, "I don't think I'm thinking at all."[6]

Have you ever tried to change a habit you have, particularly when it is an ingrained muscle memory? Was it easy to do? Now let's consider our personalities. Have you perhaps completed The Birkman® Questionnaire, the Myers-Briggs Type Indicator®, or the INSIGHT Inventory®? When we administer those questionnaires and provide results to people, we typically hear, "I'm just like that" or "People say that about me." These instruments are predicated on the idea that people do not change significantly over time. Five years ago or ten years from now, a Myers-Briggs assessment will yield nearly identical results.[7]

Our habits can hijack our behaviors. This *hijacking* frequently expresses itself in our prejudices that may be unconscious. Consider your involvement in, or observation of, debates about politics, climate change, or immigration, to mention a few recent headlines. Are people receptive, able to listen to another viewpoint, capable of moving beyond disagreement? Regrettably, our experience indicates many more thumbs down than thumbs up responses to these questions. In many cases, continually thinking and speaking about our positions on these matters, selective reading that supports our position, and accumulating cohorts who share our views all contribute to developing habits (i.e., wheel ruts) that are difficult to change.

Roger Birkman once explained that people's brains are hardwired, making change difficult. Birkman theorized that most people are 70–80% hardwired and that only 20–30% of our "free will" can be utilized to modify the wiring (i.e., neural networks) and introduce new behaviors. These new behaviors must be practiced to develop more desirable habits, and that practice is difficult.[8]

If you wish to develop yourself as a communicator and a leader, it will entail changing certain behaviors. And, if you want those behaviors to develop into more productive habits, you must practice those behaviors (build the muscle memory, so to speak). The following list describes the expectations in terms of what this book is asking you to do:

1. Commit to identifying behaviors you want to change and practice those behaviors to build a more productive skill set.
2. Commit to abandoning habits that are preventing you from reaching your goals.
3. Commit to doing the work involved to further develop and strengthen the behavior-based skills that will make you more effective as a communicator and leader.

1.3 THE PATH THROUGH THE CHAPTERS

The format that is used in the chapters that follow is:

1. We ask you to consider your own experiences with each chapter's subject. For instance, the subject of Chapter 5 is *Feedback*, where you are asked to think about impactful experiences that you have had when receiving feedback as well as what you did to facilitate those positive interactions. Next, consider instances when the feedback that you received was not impactful or helpful and what you might have done to contribute to that poor experience. You will then be asked to list behaviors that you wish to modify due to your feedback experiences.

2. The chapters then present information provided by the authors, other subject matter experts, and lessons learned from others. For instance, when receiving feedback, the chapter will present ways for mining value from feedback even when it appears to be unfair or poorly delivered.

3. At the end of each chapter, you will choose no more than two to three focus areas (feel free to write in the book or download the blank focus area template at www.jrosspub.com/CLT) that will provide the greatest impact for you to develop more effective behaviors as a communicator (Part I) and as a leader (Part II).

4. You will engage in a transformational process in Part III where you will choose no more than three of these previously identified high-priority focus areas from your work in the communication and leadership chapters that provide the greatest opportunity for improvement (see Figure 1.2). You will then transform your focus areas into goals, plans to achieve your goals, and how you will measure progress:

    *   Behavior-based goals will detail what you want to accomplish—it is important to set *SMART* (specific, measurable, achievable, relevant, and time-bound) goals. For instance, a goal of *improving team members' performance by establishing a feedback process* could entail:
        *   Preparing for conversations regarding feedback on performance by reviewing your observations and the observations of other team members
        *   Beginning feedback conversations by asking team members to assess their own performance

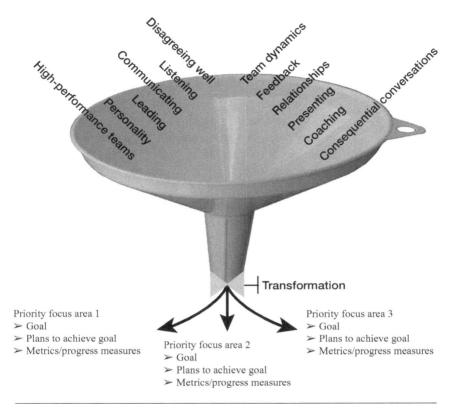

Figure 1.2 Prioritizing focus areas to goals

Priority focus area 1
➢ Goal
➢ Plans to achieve goal
➢ Metrics/progress measures

Priority focus area 2
➢ Goal
➢ Plans to achieve goal
➢ Metrics/progress measures

Priority focus area 3
➢ Goal
➢ Plans to achieve goal
➢ Metrics/progress measures

- ◘ Aligning with team members on areas of strengths, with examples of exemplary and satisfactory performance, as well as opportunities for improvement
- ◘ Developing action plans to assist with skill development
- ◘ Supporting the skill development of team members through training, job rotation, and mentoring
- ◘ Conducting regular informal conversations about progress toward outcomes
- Create plans to accomplish the goal, including milestones, a timetable, and specific activities to practice new behaviors—for instance, plans for reaching feedback goals could contain the following:
  - ◘ Meet monthly with HR for training, coaching, and obtaining ideas for improving feedback

 ▫ Meet with other team leaders monthly to discuss ideas, challenges, and successes regarding offering feedback to team members
 ▫ Attend at least one training program within six months regarding how to receive and give feedback
 ▫ Self-assess on goal achievement monthly
 ▫ Obtain feedback quarterly from team members on the impact of feedback, including what to do more of or less of and what to start doing or stop doing
 • Determine metrics to track your progress—this will include feedback from others:
 ▫ A minimum of 90% of the performance objectives of team members are achieved within an agreed-upon time
 ▫ Commitments to modify the feedback process are received within two weeks
 ▫ Obtain buy-in from team members that the process is effective in helping them improve their skills
5. In addition, Part III concludes with tools to help you develop a leadership message to transform your team into a high-performance team.

LIMITING PRIORITIES

A word of advice before proceeding with the exercises throughout this book: improving in a few key areas is better than trying to work on many goals only to be discouraged by a lack of progress due to the demands of other priorities. And, when progress is inhibited, the commitment and motivation to develop more effective behaviors drops off dramatically. Consequently, the goal of Part III is to assist you in prioritizing areas for improvement to the critical few where you are committed to develop more effective communication and leadership behaviors.

The following is an outline of the material in each part of this book—Part I: Communication, Part II: Leadership, and Part III: Transformation.

1.4   PART I: COMMUNICATION

Part I begins with an assessment of your baseline communication skills in Chapter 2. You may refer to that baseline in later chapters to help you identify and clarify focus areas. You will then complete a personality profile (Chapter 3) to identify your personality traits, how you can work with your traits, and how they can be perceived by others—both positively and negatively. In Chapter 3, you will begin to identify focus areas for improvement and continue that effort throughout the remainder of the book.

Up next is to explore communication concepts and tools including:

1. Listening
2. Giving and receiving feedback
3. Building relationships
4. How to disagree well
5. How to plan and conduct critical conversations
6. How to build effective presentations

You will have the opportunity to select or update focus areas at the end of each chapter.

Part I concludes with an opportunity for you to update and prioritize your focus areas for improvement in communication.

1.5   PART II: LEADERSHIP

With communication as a foundation, Part II focuses on leadership. Our sojourn is similar to the communication journey.

1. You will complete an assessment of your leadership skills in Chapter 10. Identify key focus areas for improvement based on the assessment, your experiences with effective leaders, and insights gained from the reading material.
2. A framework for managing team dynamics is provided in Chapter 11. Coaching is a key role for leaders of high-performing teams. Chapter 12 details tools and coaching techniques while a process for developing and leading high-performing teams is the subject of Chapter 13. Each chapter presents an opportunity to update or add to your focus areas for improvement.

1.6   PART III: TRANSFORMATION

The book concludes with Part III—your personal and team transformational goals and plans.

1. Throughout this book, you will assess your current communication and leadership skills and identify focus areas for improvement. You transform your highest-priority focus areas into goals, plans, and how you will measure progress.
2. Your *team* transformation plan is the capstone section of the book—the *team* can be your workgroup, department, division, or enterprise. Chapter 14 outlines the steps to build and implement the team transformation plan.

We will conclude the book by ensuring your development and transformation plans are aligned and integrated.

1.7   KEY TAKEAWAYS

1. An understanding of how this book is structured
2. An understanding of key terms
3. An awareness of the behavioral foundations for the recommendations throughout the book
4. An understanding of the commitment and work required to change behaviors
5. An understanding of the content of Part I: Communication, Part II: Leadership, and Part III: Transformation

Let's begin your journey to build better behavior-based communication and leadership skills!

ENDNOTES

1. "Skill Definition and Meaning." Retrieved January 22, 2022, from https://www.merriam-webster.com/dictionary/skill.
2. "Behavior Definition and Meaning." Retrieved January 22, 2022, from https://www.merriam-webster.com/dictionary/behavior.
3. Dalio, Ray. 2017. *Principals*. New York, NY. Simon & Schuster. p. 220.

4. Ramirez, Alejandro and Melissa R. Arbuckle. "Synaptic Plasticity: The Role of Learning and Unlearning in Addiction and Beyond." *Biological Psychiatry.* Retrieved December 3, 2020, from https://www.ncbi.nlm.nih.gov/pmc/articles/PMC5347979/.

5. Schwartz, Jeffrey M. and Sharon Begley. 2002. *The Mind and the Brain: Neuroplasticity and the Power of Mental Force.* New York, NY. Harper Collins. 15.

6. Finger, Mike. "Breanna Stewart a Model of Success for U.S. Women's Basketball." Retrieved August 4, 2021, from the *Houston Chronicle* at https://www.houstonchronicle.com/texas-sports-nation/tokyo-olympics/article/Breanna-Stewart-a-model-of-success-for-U-S-16363294.php?cmpid=gsa-chron-result/.

7. Randall, Ken, Mary Isaacson, and Carrie Ciro. "Validity and Reliability of the Myers-Briggs Personality Type Indicator: A Systematic Review and Meta-Analysis." *Journal of Best Practices in Health Professions Diversity*, no. 1 (Spring 2017), pp. 1–27.

8. Begley, Sharon. 2007. *Train Your Mind, Change Your Brain: How a New Science Reveals Our Extraordinary Potential to Transform Ourselves.* New York, NY. Ballantine Books. p. 24.

Part I

Communication

CHAPTER 2

FAILING TO COMMUNICATE IS NOT AN OPTION

"The single biggest problem in communication is the illusion that it has taken place."

—George Bernard Shaw

CHAPTER ROADMAP

More than likely you have encountered the truth of George Bernard Shaw's quote, wondering, "How could they have misunderstood what I meant?—I was so clear." With this in mind, the objective of this chapter is to lessen the likelihood of miscommunication by:

1. Aligning and agreeing on what we mean by communication
2. Aligning the communication process—participant's roles and responsibilities
3. Exploring the communication process and your roles and responsibilities
4. Completing an assessment of your communication skills to establish a baseline for improvement opportunities to be further clarified in subsequent chapters
5. Understanding how the virtual workplace impacts communication
6. Key takeaways

2.1 THE COMMUNICATION PROCESS

The starting point of this book is communication because, as James C. Humes reminds us, "The art of communication is the language of leadership." However, before beginning, let's define communication. *Communication* is defined, for the purposes of this book, as *a process in which you have a critical role*. To explain, this process involves:

1. The sender plans and then develops (encodes) a message.
2. The sender transmits/sends that message through a medium/channel to a receiver.
3. The receiver translates (decodes) the message.
4. The receiver encodes and transmits a response (feedback), at this point becoming a sender.
5. The original sender decodes the feedback. The process may go through another loop, depending on whether the participants are satisfied that it has fulfilled its purpose (that satisfaction may or may not be based on a valid assumption!).

As seen in Figure 2.1, when senders and receivers encode and decode messages, the results are influenced by a number of factors including their life experiences, age, gender, personality, education, and cultural background. In addition, *noise* (shown by the wavy lines) might affect how signals are formed and interpreted and can deflect the receiver's focus away from the message. Examples of noise include: physical, semantic, psychological, organizational, cultural, etc. As the communication process progresses, there are many opportunities for misunderstandings to occur. These misunderstandings can result in more work

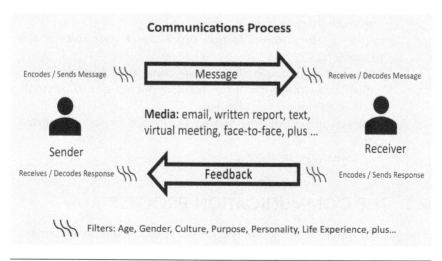

Figure 2.1   The Communications Process

to clarify what was intended, emotionally charged conversations, and unproductive conflicts.

A critical component of the communication process that is often overlooked is the medium or channel used to transmit the message. Often, the channel chosen is dictated by circumstances. For example, the CEO of an organization may choose a virtual town hall with call-in questions when announcing a new strategic initiative. In contrast, a manager may choose a face-to-face meeting with a subordinate to discuss performance relative to expectations.

Figure 2.2 depicts a notional view of the effectiveness of several communication channels. Not only do the sender and receiver play an important role in the effectiveness of communication so, too, will the channel that is chosen. The more critical the communication in terms of impact and the requirement for commitment, the more participants in the process will move up to the right-hand corner of Figure 2.2. Even the CEO, who uses the practicality of the virtual town hall, can enrich the communication by answering call-in questions and identifying the person asking the question.

IMPACT OF SOCIAL MEDIA ON COMMUNICATION

The information in Figure 2.2 helps communicators to consider the growing prevalence of social media to transmit information. Many readers may be comfortable with texting, Twitter, email, Facebook, or something similar as a means of communicating. Since these modes of communication are *word-based*, much of the richness of communication may be lost. Research shows that words can be less than 10% of the information communicated,[1] whereas more information, such as how the communicator feels, can be communicated nonverbally with voice inflection, tone, body language, gestures, eye contact, etc. While the communicator can indicate in a text that they are angry or happy, communications are more effective when they include tone, body language, and gestures. In addition, research has shown that emails are often misinterpreted and, in fact, can cause resentment and confusion in the workplace.[2] Nonetheless, the *virtual environment*—including social media tools—is a reality that requires leaders to adapt as the virtual environment becomes a bigger part of the typical work world. In recognition of this reality, several chapters will contain a subsection addressing the impact of the virtual environment on communication and leadership.

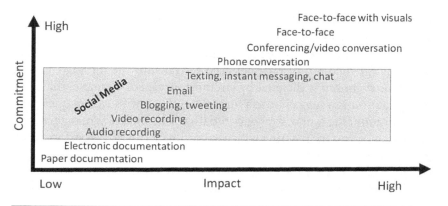

Figure 2.2 Effectiveness of communication channels

2.2 ASSESSING YOUR COMMUNICATIONS BEHAVIORS

We have defined communication as a process; now let's continue the journey. The URL for a communication behavior assessment is provided following this paragraph. Complete the questionnaire (it takes about 5 minutes) by typing or pasting the URL into your web browser:

www.jrosspub.com/CLT

After completing the questionnaire, select the *Calculate my scores* button and input your overall score here. (List the scores for each functional area in the next paragraph.)

Overall score: _____

1. **Score above 90:** Excellent! You have exceptional communication abilities, whether you are sending or receiving a message.
2. **Score between 65 and 89:** You demonstrate strong communication skills. You may occasionally have difficulties when sending or receiving communications. Examine your scores and concentrate your skill development efforts on areas with lower scores.
3. **Score below 64:** You have substantial opportunities to grow as a communicator. Make note of the sections that have the most room for growth and devote your attention to them as you progress through the book.

Input your communication process component scores below. When reviewing your scores, a score below 15 is an indication of a process area where you can improve your skill as a communicator. You will further clarify these improvement areas in subsequent chapters:

1. Planning the message: _____

2. Encoding—creating a clear, well-crafted message: _____

3. Choosing the right channel: _____

4. Decoding—receiving and interpreting a message: _____

5. Feedback: _____

Consider the scores as an indicator of skill and not an absolute measure or evaluation.

The following information is intended to aid you in identifying areas in the process where you can enhance your communication skills. As you read through the information, keep in mind that the amount of time spent on the process is proportional to the level of commitment and impact that your communication involves.

Planning your communication is important. The validity of this statement is underscored by the confusing communications we have all received. When planning communications, be sure to ask yourself, have I:

1. Clarified the purpose of the communication?
2. Clearly stated requests? Ask yourself what the receiver should do with the information when you are *just* providing information.
3. Provided the information the receiver needs to take action/ make a decision? Consider the following points when providing information:
   - *Must-know* information is required for the receiver to take action in the present.
   - *Should-know* information, while important, is not needed at the present time for the receiver to make a decision or act. It may become must-know information in the future.
   - *Nice-to-know* information can be put off without jeopardizing the receiver's ability to act.

As a general rule, include must-know information in the communication and exclude the nice-to-know information. Should-know information can be added where appropriate, but in communication, *less is more* is often preferred. Strive to be efficient when communicating as well as being effective.

Encoding entails *how* the sender wants to develop a message whereas planning is concerned with *what* the sender wants to say:

1. When encoding a message, the acronym *BIC* provides guidelines:
    *   Brief—Keep the message short and to the point
    *   Informative—The communication should inform the receiver of the purpose of the communication
    *   Clear—There should be no confusion for the receiver as to what actions are being requested
2. The adage "a picture is worth a thousand words" applies when encoding a message. Use charts, graphs, and pictures where possible.
3. Be sensitive to cultural nuances in written and verbal communication, as well as avoiding jargon.

The *channel of communication* chosen determines how the communication will be delivered. Consider the following points when you choose a channel to send your message:

1. The level of commitment you are seeking and the impact on the receiver (refer back to Figure 2.2).
2. Preference of the receiver, as to how they wish to receive communications.
3. The sensitivity of the message.
4. The need for a conversation to ensure understanding and commitment.
5. The level of detail needed to ensure understanding. There is always a hybrid approach when choosing the channel, such as sending material prior to a face-to-face meeting.

Decoding the communication is concerned with how a person receives and interprets a communication. Both the sender and receiver impact how a message is decoded:

1. **The sender**—The following points can help the sender increase the probability that the communication is interpreted as intended:
    *   Ask the receiver if the message was clear and understood (depending on the relationship with the receiver, ask the receiver to summarize their understanding of the message).

- When the channel allows for visual contact with the receiver, be aware of nonverbal cues such as body language, eye contact, and tone of voice. Are the receiver's nonverbal signals indicative of engagement, interest, and commitment, or impatience, reluctance, and a lack of interest or commitment? If so, pause to confirm that the message is being understood.
- Listen to feedback in order to try to understand rather than contemplating how to respond. Use the active listening techniques discussed in Chapter 4.
- Confirm that the receiver will fulfill a request when one is called for in the communication. Focus on what the receiver *can* do and negotiate an acceptable agreement.

2. **The receiver**—You are now decoding a communication that you have received. Feedback to the sender can be provided while decoding the communication or after developing a complete response, depending on circumstances surrounding the process—e.g., face-to-face meeting versus the need for a written response. Key points while decoding and providing feedback include:

   - Listening in order to understand rather than to respond.
   - Asking for clarification when you do not understand any part of the communication. Summarize key points to assure alignment with the sender.
   - Responding with what you can do rather than what you cannot do when a commitment is requested.
   - Keeping an open mind and avoiding the urge to prejudge the sender or discount the value of the message based on previous experiences.
   - Focusing on the *what* of the communication and not on the person sending it.
   - In a meeting situation, being straightforward and asking to reschedule when you do not have the time to give the sender the attention they deserve.

As the receiver progresses from decoding to delivering feedback, they transition from receiver to sender, and the process begins anew with planning. In many cases, the entire procedure is completed in a minute or two, but in some cases, there may be several passes through the process over a period of time.

Feedback in the communication process is an indispensable aid in confirming that the sender and receiver are aligned on the purpose of the communication (whether or not they agree is another matter). While Chapter 5 will cover the subject of feedback in detail, it is discussed briefly here in the context of the communication process. Both the receiver and sender of a communication give feedback:

1. **Receiving feedback**—Most conversations and training about feedback focuses on how to *provide* feedback with far less emphasis on how to *receive* feedback. Learning how to receive feedback is just as important as learning how to give feedback:

   - When receiving feedback, listen in order to *understand* rather than *respond.*
   - Focus on mining value from feedback, regardless of whether the feedback seems unfair, inaccurate, or poorly delivered. Remember, you don't have to accept feedback and act on the feedback you receive, but listening is important.
   - Focus on the *what* of the feedback and not on *who* provides the feedback.
   - Ask questions to clarify the purpose or expectations of the person sending the communication when the purpose and expectations are not clear.
   - Ask the sender if you have met their needs when you are responding to a request for information.

2. **Giving feedback**—This is an opportunity for people who are engaged in the communication process to clarify the purpose of the communication, to express their expectations, and to confirm or negotiate commitments. Feedback is usually solicited, unsolicited, or scheduled, as in a job performance evaluation. Listed here are guidelines for providing feedback that is relative to these situations:

   - Provide *SMART* Feedback:
     - **S**pecific—Feedback should be specific in the sense that there is no confusion as to what is meant. Telling someone to be more assertive is not specific.
     - **M**easurable—There should be an intended outcome that can be assessed or measured.
     - **A**ttainable—The feedback should have an expected outcome that is attainable or achievable given the receiver's social, economic, or cultural resources and time available.

◻ **Relevant**—The feedback should be relevant to the receiver, such as improving performance in the work environment, and/or meaningful to the receiver in improving relationships, such as achieving a goal, etc.

◻ **Time-bound**—There should be a time frame when an outcome is to be achieved.

• Feedback is a conversation that helps assure:
  ◻ The receiver understands the feedback—and not just the words but also the feelings behind the words and the cultural context, so differences in cultural norms do not mask understanding.
  ◻ There is alignment on expectations.
  ◻ Expectations are understood and commitments are agreed upon.

2.3 COMMUNICATING IN THE VIRTUAL ENVIRONMENT

Communication opportunities and challenges in the virtual world are not new and extend back to the 1980s.[3] The use of tools and techniques that support the virtual world has accelerated since then due to:

1. Globalization of economies and work has necessitated more efficient communication. The bedrock of more efficient communication is internet-based communication tools and techniques. Globalization has also been a catalyst leading to a more diverse and collaborative workforce.[4]

2. Busy lifestyles, work-life balance considerations, and smart devices that open a world of information-sharing opportunities have reduced the priority of work in people's lives. These trends have necessitated more efficient and faster communication.[5]

3. The COVID-19 pandemic required more work be conducted away from centralized office space to home offices, or anywhere there is an internet connection, including airports, coffee shops, hotels, etc. Employers are becoming more comfortable that productivity can be maintained in the virtual environment, allowing many employees to work virtually or provide a hybrid approach with working virtually and at other times coming to a centralized office.[6]

4. The proliferation of smartphones with applications that provide access to almost unlimited information, ranging from weather, restaurant menus, games, and all types of social media, have blurred the distinction between work life and personal life.[7]

These trends support the conclusion that virtual tools and techniques are here to stay and will likely increase. The question becomes whether the widespread use of internet tools and techniques will benefit companies and employees. The evidence is unequivocal. It depends! The research is not conclusive. Many believe that the tools and techniques inherent in the virtual world are beneficial:

1. The global economy and a dispersed workforce can communicate quickly to solve problems, access information, and collaborate on new ideas.[8]
2. Using virtual teams can increase productivity, with some organizations seeing gains up to 43% among virtual teams compared to non-virtual teams.[9]
3. Internet-based applications provide organizations a platform for job postings outside the company website and allow access to potential employees' information on LinkedIn, Facebook, etc., that speed up the recruitment effort.[10]
4. Internet-based tools provide a means to communicate with customers, vendors, and other stakeholders anywhere in the world.[11]

Others say:

1. Easy access to online tools and techniques brings a multitude of distractions. Many complain that the preponderance of texts with senders expecting instant responses is distracting.[12]
2. Social media can become addictive, promulgating new terms including *nomophobia*[13] and *social media reversion*[14] when people cannot self-regulate and thereby spend enormous amounts of time at work on nonproductive activities involving social media tools and techniques.
3. There is an increasing amount of cyberbullying and offensive content.[15]
4. There is an increased risk of the organizations' data being hacked when social media is used on company equipment.[16]

Assuming that the virtual work environment is here to stay, the question becomes: What should organizations and their employees do about communication in the virtual workplace? The communication process shown in Figure 2.1 is relevant regardless of whether people are in the physical or virtual world. That is to say, in either environment:

1. There is still a sender and receiver of information.
2. The sender and receiver both encode and decode messages.
3. Messages are delivered through a channel.
4. As messages are encoded, sent, received, decoded, and feedback is provided, there are opportunities for miscommunication. Biases, cultural differences, language differences, and *noise* can cause miscommunication, strain relationships, produce stress, and result in unproductive time being necessary to realign intentions.

There are two differences as to how the communication process can be practiced in the virtual world when compared to the physical world. One difference is somewhat minor; the other difference more significant:

1. Channels in the strictly virtual world are limited to internet-based applications, including email, video conferencing, texting, Snapchat, Twitter, etc. It is important to remember that the actual and virtual worlds are not mutually exclusive. Numerous firms take a hybrid approach with the team spending time in both spaces.
2. There is a greater need for individual responsibility when using internet-based tools appropriately—especially social media—and a greater need for organizations to provide efficient and effective tools and guidelines to facilitate efficient and effective communication in the virtual world.

We will discuss opportunities and problems for communication and leadership in the virtual world throughout this book, including listening, relationship building, and leadership in the virtual environment, to mention a few.

2.4 RECONFIRMING THE PATH FORWARD

Let's pause for a moment to review what you can expect going forward. In this chapter you established a baseline of your skills used in the communication process. In future chapters you will develop focus areas for improving and developing your behavior-based skills as a communicator and leader. You may find opportunities to refer back to your baseline communication process skills to help clarify areas for improvement. It is possible that you will discover many areas for improvement. Consequently, you will be asked to prioritize focus areas by the most impactful to avoid diluting your efforts or becoming discouraged by a lack of progress.

2.5   KEY TAKEAWAYS

Let's summarize to ensure everything is in place before we continue:

1. You understand the components of the communication process
2. You have established a baseline of your communication process skills that may be used to clarify opportunities for improving behavior-based skills identified in future chapters
3. You understand how the virtual environment impacts the communication process

ENDNOTES

1. Belludi, Nagesh. "Albert Mehrabian's 7-38-55 Rule of Personal Communication." Retrieved February 22, 2021 from *Right Attitudes* at https://www.rightattitudes.com/2008/10/04/7-38-55-rule-personal -communication/.
2. "CPP Survey: 64% Cite #Email as a Source of #Workplace Confusion, Resentment." Retrieved February 22, 2021, from *Sendmail* at https://www.prnewswire.com/news-releases/sendmail -cpp-survey-64-cite-email-as-source-of-workplace-confusion -resentment-211802791.html.
3. Ancona, D. and D. Caldwell. 1988. "Beyond Task and Maintenance: Defining External Functions in Groups." *Group and Organizational Studies* 13, no. 4, pp. 476–494.
4. Ifigeneia, Mylona and Amanatidis Dimitrios. "Globalization, Social Media and Public Relations: A Necessary Relationship for the Future?" Retrieved on June 22, 2021, from *Knowledge E* at https://knepublishing.com/index.php/KnE-Social/article/view/ 3546/7438.

5. Park Point University Online. 2019. "Using Technology to Improve Communication at Work." Retrieved June 15, 2021, from *CMS WiRE* at https://www.cmswire.com/digital-workplace/using-technology-to-improve-communication-at-work/.

6. Blanchard, Anita. "The Effects of COVID-19 on Virtual Working Within Online Groups." Retrieved June 5, 2021, from *Group Processes and Intergroup Relations* at https://journals.sagepub.com/doi/full/10.1177/1368430220983446.

7. Cleary, John. "The Impact of Social Media at the Workplace." Retrieved March 4, 2021 from *In House Legal* at https://inhouse-legal.eu/in-house-managment/social-media-workplace/.

8. Bennett, K., M. Pitt, and M. Owers. "Workplace Impact of Social Networking." Retrieved June 18, 2021, from *The School of Built Environment, Liverpool John Moores University* at https://citeseerx.ist.psu.edu/viewdoc/download?doi=10.1.1.467.8755&rep=rep1&type=pdf#page=68.

9. Trees, Lauren. 2020. "Virtual Collaboration: Rules of the Road." Retrieved March 12, 2021 from *American Productivity & Quality Center* at https://www.apqc.org/system/files/resource-file/2020-11/K011065_Virtual_Collaboration_Rules_Road_Report.pdf.

10. "Advantages and Disadvantages of Social Media at Work." Retrieved May 23, 2021, from *Indeed for Employers* at https://www.indeed.com/hire/c/info/what-are-the-advantages-and-disadvantages-of-social-media.

11. Kelleher, David. "5 Problems with Social Networking in the Workplace." Retrieved December 20, 2020, from *Cerait* at https://www.cerait.com/blog/5-problems-social-networking-workplace.

12. Zimmerman, Kaytie. "Is Your Cell Phone Killing Your Productivity at Work?" Retrieved June 25, 2021, from *Forbes* at https://www.forbes.com/sites/kaytiezimmerman/2017/03/26/is-your-cell-phone-killing-your-productivity-at-work/?sh=135c44ad605c.

13. Ibid.

14. Elgan, Mike. "Social Media Addiction is a Bigger Problem than You Think." Retrieved May 28, 2021, from *Computerworld* at https://www.computerworld.com/article/3014439/social-media-addiction-is-a-bigger-problem-than-you-think.html?page=2.

15. Todd, Steve. "25 Problems with Social Media in the Workplace (Employee and Employer Adverse Effects)." Retrieved May 15, 2021, from *Open Sourced Workplace* at https://www.open sourcedworkplace.com/news/25-problems-with-social-media-in -the-workplace-employee-and-employer-adverse-effects.

16. "Advantages and Disadvantages of Social Media at Work." Retrieved May 23, 2021, from *Indeed for Employers* at https:// www.indeed.com/hire/c/info/what-are-the-advantages-and -disadvantages-of-social-media.

CHAPTER 3

WHO ARE YOU? YOUR PERSONALITY TRAITS

"He who knows others is wise. He who knows himself is enlightened."

—Lao Tzu

CHAPTER ROADMAP

The objective of this chapter is to help you understand your personality strengths—how you are *wired* in a sense, and how your personality traits affect the way you transmit (i.e., encode messages) and receive communications (i.e., decode messages). With that self-awareness, you'll be better prepared to leverage your personality's strengths, adapt your strengths to accommodate the personality traits of others, and manage stressful situations that may cause you to overuse your strengths. The following list is a roadmap for navigating this chapter:

1. An introduction to personality traits and tools
2. The INSIGHT Inventory®
3. Personality traits and their characteristics
4. Understanding your personality traits
5. How to leverage your personality traits and when to flex your strengths to accommodate the traits of others
6. Identifying your focus areas for improvement
7. An opportunity for a team to generate a map showing the relative position of its members' personality traits
8. Key takeaways for this chapter

3.1　INTRODUCTION

Benjamin Franklin pointed out in *Poor Richard's Almanac*, "There are three things extremely hard: steel, a diamond, and to know one's self." If that is the case, how do you come to know yourself as expressed in your personality traits? You can start by asking others for feedback. While this input can be beneficial, it is inherently unreliable and subjective.[1] Recognizing the importance of understanding how personality traits influence behavior and because of the difficulty of obtaining objective and reliable feedback, a number of assessments have been developed, including the Myers-Briggs Type Indicator®, the Birkman Method®, and the INSIGHT Inventory®. These instruments have been shown to have reasonable statistical reliability (i.e., the instruments yield the same results over multiple trials) and be statistically valid (i.e., the instrument measures what it was designed to measure).

3.2　THE INSIGHT INVENTORY®—AN OVERVIEW

The INSIGHT Inventory® is composed of four *traits*, or scales, with the characteristics of people who have different behavioral *preferences* on each trait, along with considerations for communication with people with similar and opposite preferences.[2]

To further clarify terms used in the INSIGHT Inventory®, a trait, such as Influencing, describes how people express thoughts, ideas, and assert themselves. There are preferred behaviors within the traits—and for Influencing, the preferences are Direct and Indirect.

> Information in this chapter is reprinted with permission of the INSIGHT Institute and is adapted from Patrick Handley's *INSIGHT . . . Into Your Unique Personality Strengths* (Kansas City, MO, Insight Institute Press, 2019).

The following list includes brief descriptions of the four traits:

1. **Influencing**—Measures how people express thoughts, present ideas, and assert themselves. The two opposite preferences are Direct and Indirect:
   - *Direct*: more assertive, candid, sometimes blunt, and takes charge

- *Indirect*: less assertive, tactful, diplomatic, approachable, and unassuming

Have you had challenges communicating with people who are Direct? Indirect? Think about your experiences for a moment. Some how-to recommendations for communicating with people of opposite preferences will be presented in the next section.

2. **Responding**—Measures how people approach and respond to others, particularly in groups of people, and how people express their emotions and sociability. The two opposite preferences are Outgoing and Reserved:

   - *Outgoing*: Talkative, animated, expressive, and share emotions openly
   - *Reserved*: Introspective, keeps emotions private, more energized alone or in small groups, thinks problems through alone to clarify feelings, and less expressive with gestures

Consider how to respond to a person who is Reserved or one who is Outgoing. Is it best to be expressive and talkative or a bit quiet and laid back? Answers to these questions are in the next section.

3. **Pacing**—Measures the speed in which people make decisions and take actions. The two opposite preferences are Urgent and Steady:

   - *Urgent*: Quick and fast-acting; considers a few important options before deciding
   - *Steady*: Patient, deliberate, and easygoing

What speed of action or decision making does the person you are communicating with prefer? Should you move fast and decide quickly or provide more time for deliberation and exploration of options? Strategies for working with Urgent and/or Steady people are presented in the next section.

4. **Organizing**—Measures how people structure their time, organize tasks, and handle detail. The two opposite preferences are Unstructured and Precise:

   - *Unstructured*: Flexible, nonconforming, and unplanned
   - *Precise*: Structured, conforming, and planned

When communicating with people, consider how much organization or structure they prefer. For example, should ideas be presented in big-picture, broad-overview terms or with many details and supporting facts? Ideas on how to work with Unstructured and Precise preferences are presented in the next section.

In the following pages, you will be led through exercises to position yourself in each of the four personality traits based on your respective preferences. Once finished, you will have a profile of your personality traits as shown in Figure 3.1, presented as an example.

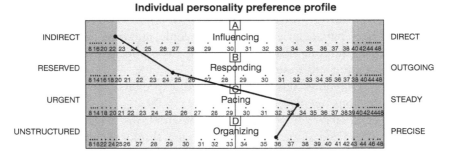

Figure 3.1   Individual personality trait profile

3.3   UNDERSTANDING YOUR PERSONALITY TRAITS

The following sections contain detailed descriptions of the four personality traits, including behavioral preferences, strengths, and stress behaviors. Utilize the information to determine your relative position on the preferences for the four traits in the figures provided. At the end of each trait, there are suggestions for communicating with others whose preferences differ from yours.

GO WITH YOUR STRENGTHS

Going with your strengths[3] rather than working to overcome weaknesses is an axiom of this book. Seek work and an environment that will allow you to leverage your strengths. Be aware that we are not advocating that you change your preferences as you read through the suggestions that follow. Rather, be prepared to *flex* your preferred behaviors to a degree. In fact, it may be necessary to move to a different environment when your strengths are not valued.

In addition, there are tips for avoiding or managing stress-related behaviors. Stress behaviors are usually triggered when needs are not met. The first step toward managing stress behaviors is to become aware when you are engaging in them. Methods for avoiding or managing stress behaviors that apply to all the personality traits include:

1. Avoid situations where the needs of your preferred behaviors are not met.
2. Inform others about your preferences so that they do not misinterpret your behaviors. While you may be able to flex your behavior to a degree, request that they respect your preferred behaviors.
3. Seek activities that are aligned with the needs of your preferences, including hobbies, sports, and social activities.

Numerous recommendations contained in the upcoming material may strike a chord with you. You may discover behaviors that you should start doing, do more of, or do less of. You may feel that some behaviors should be abandoned because they hinder your effectiveness as a communicator. At the end of this chapter, you will identify two focus areas where changing your behaviors will improve how you communicate.

1. **Influencing (Scale A)**—As the name implies, Influencing refers to how people express thoughts and ideas. How people assert themselves has an impact on how they influence others. As a word of caution, the Influencing trait does not measure self-esteem, confidence, power, or whether a person is successful. The two opposite preferences for Influencing are Direct and Indirect:
   - *Direct*: A Direct individual goes straight to the point. They are usually forthright and assertive. Direct people come across as confident and forceful. They like to tackle disputes and debate disagreements openly. They frequently *tell* rather than *ask*:
     □ *Strengths*: The Direct individual takes the initiative, particularly in circumstances that require control and clarity of direction. In addition, they can bring out ambiguous or concealed issues and restate them in a bottom-line, concise way.
     □ *Stress behaviors*: When Direct people are unable to influence others, the issue is unclear, or they cannot express their thoughts (i.e., their preferred behaviors are blocked), they are prone to becoming frustrated and stressed. Direct individuals may overuse their strengths in stressful situations by being demanding, argumentative, or too pushy.

   Do you know people who prefer to be Direct (i.e., they state their position on issues candidly and frankly)?

- *Indirect*: Indirect people prefer to be tactful and courteous. They are accessible because they tend to be less forceful. They tend to *ask* rather than *tell*, and they approach people with a supportive and courteous attitude. The Indirect person would rather negotiate than debate differences. In addition, they may express their opinions modestly and occasionally understate their viewpoint and beliefs:
    - *Strengths*: Rather than taking command, the Indirect person prefers to negotiate and encourage dialogue. They will frequently keep their concerns to themselves, allowing others to speak. They seek to avoid controversy by carefully framing their remarks to avoid offending others.
    - *Stress behaviors*: Indirect people can become frustrated when others want to rigorously debate disagreements or when they are drawn into arguments. As a result, Indirect individuals avoid such situations or concede when they are not truly in agreement.

Do you know people whose preference is to be Indirect?

Given the descriptions presented here, what is your preference? Locate yourself on the continuum shown in Figure 3.2.

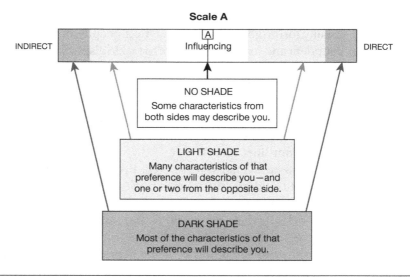

Figure 3.2   Influencing

Individuals who fall at the extremes of the continuum shown for all of the trait preferences are likely to exhibit more prominent characteristics of that preference and face greater difficulty adapting their behaviors. Individuals who place themselves closer to the center of the continuum may find it easier to adapt their behavior in order to work with the preferences of others. Regardless of where you fall on the continuum, the ideas after each preference may be beneficial in highlighting the areas in which you could improve as a communicator:

- Communicating with opposites—Direct and Indirect:
  - When a Direct attempts to persuade an Indirect, the Direct person can focus on being less demanding and forceful than they would ordinarily be. The Indirect may perceive the assertive approach as pressure and find ways to avoid or terminate interactions. In addition, a strong voice, assertive attitude, and telling people what to do may overwhelm Indirect people, causing them to withdraw. The Direct individual can practice being more tactful when interacting with Indirect individuals. Direct people can tone down their preference to debate differences and take charge because the Indirect individual may disengage and assume that the Direct person is not interested in their input.
  - When an Indirect talks with a Direct, the Indirect person can practice expressing their views and opinions more assertively since Direct people value conviction and self-assuredness. The Indirect person should be prepared with data and examples when meeting to influence a Direct individual because Direct people prefer to challenge and confront differences. Indirect people can also focus on the *what* and *why* in conversations rather than the person.

We can frame the communication between a person with Direct and Indirect preferences using the communication process described in Chapter 2. For example, assume John is the manager of a project that needs more resources to complete an important task on schedule. Alice is a senior manager in another department who controls how resources are allocated among projects including John's. John has a preference for a more direct approach when influencing people whereas Alice's preference is to be Indirect. Figure 3.3 demonstrates how the communication process described in Chapter 2 could apply to how John and Alice communicate.

John

Alice

Planning:

1. Before meeting with Alice, send her information that justifies diverting resources from other projects.
2. Be prepared to accept a need for additional meetings to provide additional information.

Encoding:

1. When meeting with Alice, be less candid and forceful than normal.
2. Be willing to explore options rather than putting Alice in a situation where you expect a yes or no answer immediately.

Channel of communication:

1. Face-to-face meeting.
2. Prior to the meeting, send Alice information she will need to make a decision.

Decoding:

1. Paraphrase Alice's concerns to ensure you understand them and find alignment on issues and a path forward.
2. Be aware of Alice's nonverbal cues, such as body language, eye contact, and tone of voice that may indicate whether she agrees or disagrees.

Feedback:

1. Look for the *value* in what Alice is saying, rather than listening to *respond* to Alice's remarks to convince her to comply with your request.
2. Summarize the meeting to assure alignment on the next steps. Let Alice know that you appreciate her willingness to discuss your needs.

Planning:

1. Be prepared with data and examples to identify the issues when meeting with John.
2. Ensure John understands how various projects contribute to meeting the needs of the organization and explore ways for his project to create more value.

Encoding:

1. When responding to John or expressing a point of view, be more expressive with gestures, eye contact, and voice than normal.
2. Ensure John understands how various projects contribute to meeting the needs of the organization and explore ways for his project to create more value.

Channel of communication:

1. Face-to-face meeting.

Decoding:

1. Paraphrase John's position to demonstrate to him you understand what he needs and why he needs it.
2. Ask questions to clarify points that are not clear and to help John reframe things in a more positive way.

Feedback:

1. Ask John to assess whether his needs trump the needs of other projects in creating value to the organization.
2. Summarize the results of the meeting, next steps, and thank John for the time he has taken to prepare for the meeting and his openness to explore options.

Figure 3.3   Mapping personality preferences to the communication process

The example shown in Figure 3.3 can be applied to the additional personality trait preferences described below.

2. **Responding (Scale B)**—This trait measures how individuals approach and respond to others, particularly in groups, and how they express their emotions and sociability. The Responding trait does not assess shyness, capacity to communicate, interest in other people, or a need for time to be alone. Outgoing and Reserved are opposite preferences:

- *Outgoing*: As you might guess, Outgoing individuals are talkative, lively, expressive, and openly share their feelings. They are energized by human interaction and participation in a variety of activities. In addition, they prefer to discuss issues with others in order to clarify their feelings and frequently employ gestures and facial expressions when speaking:
  - *Strengths*: Outgoing individuals put others at ease by instilling a sense of importance in those they encounter. Other people are important to Outgoing individuals. They exhibit their preference by being engaged and informed about the personal struggles of others.
  - *Stress behaviors*: When Outgoing individuals lack interaction with others or lose group support and reinforcement, they may talk excessively and try too hard to gain approval or act in an overly friendly manner.

  Take a moment to consider people you know. Are there people who have an Outgoing preference?

- *Reserved*: Reserved individuals are contemplative, keep their feelings private, and are more energized alone or in small groups. They reason things out on their own to clarify their emotions and are less expressive with gestures. They are more comfortable talking with others on an individual basis and get energized when they are alone and away from activities. When they speak, they tend to use a limited number of gestures and facial expressions:
  - *Strengths*: Reserved people pay close attention to what others say and allow others to speak more than they do themselves. They exhibit fewer facial expressions and emotional displays, frequently defusing emotionally charged situations.

▫ *Stress behaviors*: When confronted with an overwhelming number of people or when under pressure to speak more, Reserved individuals may withdraw and become overly silent or withhold input even when it is needed.

Do you know people who are Reserved in how they interact with others?

Given the descriptions presented here, what is your preference? Locate yourself on the continuum shown in Figure 3.4.

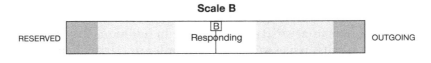

Figure 3.4   Responding

- Communicating with opposites—Outgoing and Reserved:
  - ▫ When an Outgoing person speaks with a Reserved person, the Outgoing person can encourage the Reserved person to speak more by asking open-ended questions because yes or no inquiries are likely to elicit a one-word response. The Outgoing person can maintain awareness and modulate their Outgoing nature by talking less than they would normally. Reserved individuals will most likely allow Outgoing individuals to fill in the quiet space with their own voice.
  - ▫ When a Reserved person speaks with an Outgoing person, they can practice being more lively and enthusiastic than they typically would since Outgoing individuals are more at ease with enthusiasm and excitement. The Reserved person can spend time getting to know Outgoing people by exhibiting photographs of family, hobbies, and pets at their workplace. The information given by these images will make it easier to share further personal information with others.
3. **Pacing (Scale C)**—Pacing measures the speed at which individuals make decisions and take action. The Pacing trait does not assess the quality of decisions made, an individual's productivity, the proper manner to accomplish things, or the amount of

energy people put into their work. The two opposite preferences are Urgent and Steady:

- *Urgent*: Urgent people get things done by acting quickly and prefer short-term projects requiring quick responses. They operate in a fast-paced, hasty manner and weigh only a few critical choices before making a decision:
    - *Strengths*: Urgent individuals take actions quickly when opportunities arise that require immediate decisions. They swiftly discard alternatives that appear to confuse issues or delay action.
    - *Stress behaviors*: Urgent people can get frustrated and impatient or make decisions impulsively when there is either a lack of action, a slow decision-making process, or changes in decisions that cause delays.

    Are there people you know who make decisions quickly and get impatient if there is a lack of action?

- *Steady*: Steady individuals are patient, deliberate, and easygoing. They succeed by persistence and enjoy longer term projects with calculated responses. They work at an even pace and consistent style, while making decisions cautiously after examining all available options:
    - *Strengths*: Steady individuals postpone decisions until better opportunities present themselves. They patiently remain receptive to options that have potential but may have been dismissed by others.
    - *Stress behaviors*: Steady individuals may find methods to delay decisions or actions when under pressure to make quick decisions, meet last-minute deadlines, or deal with numerous interruptions.

    Take a moment to consider people you know. Are there people who have a Steady preference?

Given the descriptions presented here, what is your preference? Locate yourself on the continuum shown in Figure 3.5.

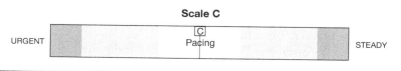

Scale C

URGENT   Pacing   STEADY

Figure 3.5 Pacing

- Communication with opposites—Urgent and Steady
    - When an Urgent communicates with a Steady, the Urgent person can work to align on desired objectives before meeting with a Steady person who prefers additional time to consider options before making a decision or acting. Concentrating on what *can* be accomplished, the Urgent individual can demonstrate flexibility and negotiate commitments with a Steady individual. In addition, the Urgent individual can communicate scheduling or time constraints to a Steady person as far in advance as possible, allowing the Steady person time to prepare. The Urgent individual should share information and often engage in order to ensure that the Steady individual has the information necessary to make decisions.
    - When a Steady communicates with an Urgent, try hard to agree on specific results because the Urgent person prefers to get things done quickly and wants to achieve more success. The Steady individual can concentrate on what actions can be taken and what is required before proceeding further. Keep an Urgent person informed when more time is required to incorporate new information before a decision can be made. The Steady person can communicate concepts succinctly and focus on *must-know* information because Urgent people are likely to disengage when details obscure critical points.
4. **Organizing (Scale D)**—The Organizing trait measures preferences people have for structuring their time, organizing tasks, and handling details. The Organizing trait does not measure quality, creativity, or the ability to organize. The two opposite preferences are Unstructured and Precise:
    - *Unstructured*: Unstructured individuals are adaptable, nonconforming, and will begin projects without reading all the instructions. They prefer less direction—in other words, simply provide them with the objectives. They defer arranging and paying attention to detail and employ unconventional approaches.
        - *Strengths*: The Unstructured individual discovers and implements innovative ways for accomplishing goals.

They work through disorder and complete tasks in settings that may bother others.

□ *Stress behaviors*: When too many norms and procedures are enforced or when there is a lack of flexibility or support for doing things differently, Unstructured individuals may work around rules and neglect details and timetables that are critical to others.

Take a moment to consider people you know. Are there people who prefer very little structure?

• *Precise*: Precise individuals are well-structured and conforming. They tend to organize details in a timely and complete manner and carry out activities according to established procedures. They prefer well-defined and fairly predictable plans and begin projects only after reading all instructions:

□ *Strengths*: Precise individuals can restore order and structure to disorganized situations and identify methods to enhance procedures and rules that aid in the smooth execution of tasks.

□ *Stress behaviors*: Precise individuals may get more organized than needed and attend to minute details. They may overwhelm others with details and lists when in ambiguous situations where there is a lack of organization or planning or unpredictable changes.

Do you know people who are Precise in how they organize work and planning?

Given the descriptions presented here, what is your preference for Organizing? Locate yourself on the continuum shown in Figure 3.6:

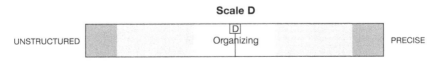

Scale D

UNSTRUCTURED   Organizing   PRECISE

Figure 3.6 Organizing

• Communicating with opposites—Unstructured and Precise:

□ When an Unstructured person communicates with a Precise, the Unstructured individual can practice being punctual and ordered since Precise individuals respect these abilities. Before attempting to persuade Precise individuals, gather information and details in a more systematic manner than an Unstructured person would ordinarily choose; utilize notes and refer to them as required. Respect a Precise individual's choice for processes and plans. When suggesting an unconventional approach, be prepared to discuss costs, advantages, and risk management techniques.

◻ When a Precise communicates with an Unstructured, the Precise person can place a greater emphasis on big picture results than they would otherwise. With sufficient risk reduction, the Precise individual may remain receptive to novel and unproven ideas. Assign a goal to the Unstructured individual and be receptive to their technique of planning as they go. Inform the Unstructured individual about the knowledge required to ensure that an unconventional approach remains within risk tolerances.

Transfer your perceived trait preferences from Figures 3.2, 3.4, 3.5, and 3.6 to Figure 3.7. This will help you view them from a holistic perspective. What insights do you gain from the profile in terms of how you would communicate with people who have different preferences?

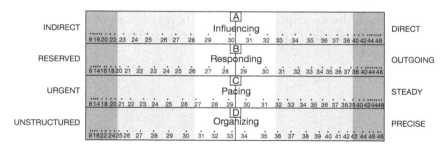

Figure 3.7 Your personality preference profile

3.4   FOCUS AREAS FOR IMPROVEMENT

You have identified your preferred behaviors for each of the personality traits. You have an understanding of what you believe to be so. The question now is, "So what?" What do you do with the understanding of your personality traits gained by completing the exercises in the previous section?

Think about how your behavioral preferences facilitate or hinder your communications, particularly with people who have opposite preferences. Do certain behaviors that you have stand out? Behaviors you should do more of, do less of, or stop doing because they undermine the effectiveness of your communications? Do opportunities jump out at you in the sense of behaviors you should start doing to improve as a communicator?

Choose no more than two behaviors where you want to focus on change. In this chapter, however, focus on how your trait preferences enhance or diminish your effectiveness as a communicator.

FOCUS AREAS FOR CHAPTER 3

Focus area 1—Describe an important behavior-based trait preference area where you want to improve (e.g., I am an Indirect person so when speaking to a Direct person, use more eye contact and gestures: be prepared to debate issues):

_____

_____

_____

Focus area 2—Describe an important behavior-based trait preference area where you want to improve:

_____

_____

_____

While you have captured focus areas for this chapter on the previous page, we encourage you to go to www.jrosspub.com/CLT where you can download a blank form to keep track of your focus areas created in exercises throughout this book. The template will prove invaluable in your work to prioritize focus areas in Chapters 9, 13, and 14.

3.5   IMPROVING TEAM PERFORMANCE

You completed exercises to identify your specific personality preferences in Section 3.3. Members of a team can complete an INSIGHT Inventory® to obtain a *team map*. Personality traits and their associated behavioral preferences can either enhance or detract from team success. Consequently, understanding team members' preferences helps accelerate reaching the status of a high-performing team (as described in Chapter 13). The INSIGHT Institute provides a team map that illustrates team members' behavioral preferences for those who complete the INSIGHT Inventory®. Figure 3.8 shows an example of a team map (there is a cost for each team member that completes the INSIGHT Inventory®). Note: if you take the actual INSIGHT Inventory® personality profile, whether as an individual or part of a team exercise, notice if your *perceived* placements on the four trait continuums from Section 3.3 are the same as your *actual* scores. This may adjust your focus areas for improvement that you just listed as typically it is better to work with your actual scores than how you might perceive yourself.

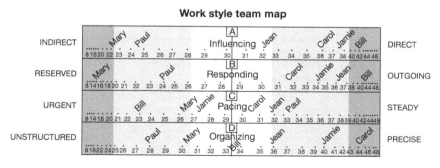

Figure 3.8   Sample Report—INSIGHT Inventory® work style team map

Referring to Figure 3.8, consider:

1. What challenges can you envision when Bill (Direct and Outgoing) communicates with Mary (Indirect and Reserved)?
2. How can Carol (Precise) adapt her behaviors to communicate with Paul (more Unstructured)?

A team map may be used in team meetings or among individuals to identify preferences, areas for improvement in communication and understanding, and strategies to boost performance. The INSIGHT Inventory® can be accessed using the URL provided following this paragraph. On the INSIGHT website, more materials and tools are accessible, including name tests that indicate team member preferences and activities that promote greater collaboration:

www.insightinventory.com

Bear in mind that trait preferences are like vitamins. Vitamin needs vary by individual. One individual requires 76 mg of vitamin C, whereas another requires 24 mg. This is not to say that one individual is better or worse than the other, just that their requirements are distinct. The same is true for behavioral preferences. Each preference has advantages, and in certain circumstances, you may need to be flexible to accommodate the preference of others or at least be aware of your preferences when communicating with others.

3.6   KEY TAKEAWAYS

1. How our brains are *wired* has a significant impact on how we behave in the communication process (e.g., what and how we send and receive communications).
2. Although to some extent, our brains are *hard wired*, we all have the ability to adapt our behaviors when communicating with others.
3. Learn to make an assessment of your personality traits and underlying behavioral preferences.
4. Understanding that your ability to adapt your behaviors is enhanced when you understand your personality traits and supporting behavioral preferences, along with how they influence the way you relate to others.

5. Completing the assessments can help you understand your personality traits and provide guidance on how to relate to others with similar and dissimilar behavioral preferences.
6. You have identified behavioral-based focus areas based on insights gained from completing the exercises in this chapter.
7. You have decided whether to use the INSIGHT team map to understand how to communicate with similar and dissimilar personality preferences.

ENDNOTES

1. Vazire, S. February 2010. "Who Knows What About a Person? The Self-Other Knowledge Asymmetry (SOKA) Model." *Journal of Personality and Social Psychology* 98, no. 2.
2. Handley, Patrick. 2019. *INSIGHT . . . into your unique personality strengths*. Kansas City, MO. Insight Institute Press.
3. Rath, Tom and Barry Conchie. 2008. *Strengths Based Leadership: Great Leaders, Teams, and Why People Follow*. New York, NY. Gallup Press. p. 23.

CHAPTER **4**

LISTEN BETTER TO SUCCEED

---

*"Most people do not listen with the intent to understand;
they listen with the intent to reply."*

—Stephen Covey

CHAPTER ROADMAP

In Chapter 2 you were introduced to the communications process. In this chapter we will focus on improving the communications process by developing your listening and questioning skills. The following list describes the roadmap we will follow:

1. Defining the benefits of listening and questioning
2. Listening instead of hearing
3. Sharpening your listening skills
4. Understanding the barriers to listening effectively
5. Asking better questions
6. Identifying focus areas for improvement
7. Reviewing key takeaways from this chapter

4.1 THE BENEFITS OF IMPROVED LISTENING AND QUESTIONING

Improving your listening and questioning skills will help you to become a stronger communicator and leader. Sharpening your listening and questioning skills can make the difference between a mediocre leader and a transformational leader—someone who can truly make a difference. The benefits of better listening and questioning include the following:

1. Listening better and asking better follow-up questions enhances your knowledge, thereby enhancing your power in a relationship. Often, just listening better gives you benefits because you can focus on what is being said, thereby gaining clarity. You can ask questions to clarify information and to obtain a better understanding of the person, the idea, or the situation.

2. Listening can give you new perspectives, which will help resolve conflict or provide insight to someone's actions or words. Not everyone can express themselves explicitly, but by listening carefully, you may pick up on a perspective or point of view that may clarify a point of misunderstanding.

3. Enhanced listening and questioning will save time and money by reducing mistakes or unnecessary work due to misunderstandings. Sometimes, more often than people would like to admit, actions are taken that they *thought* they heard and those actions lead to extra effort or to mistakes.

4. Listening will reduce conflicts by creating a better understanding of differing points of views and by uncovering hidden agendas or motives.

5. Improving your listening and questioning skills can contribute to your personal development by enhancing your ability to handle interpersonal relationships with empathy, thereby leading to improvements in your patience, confidence, and empathy.

6. Better listening and questioning will help to develop trust and respect. People notice when you listen, and it will help them develop an attitude that you can be trusted because you understand, or at least are willing to try to understand.

7. Listening and questioning can reduce or eliminate the *noise* that can occur in the communications process. As discussed in Chapter 2, noise hinders effective communications. Noise can be introduced by any number of barriers (refer back to Figure 2.1).

8. Increased focus toward listening and questioning leads to better conversations, and better conversations lead to better relationships.

4.2   LISTENING INSTEAD OF HEARING

"Listening looks easy, but it's not simple. Every head is a world."

—Cuban Proverb

Hearing is a biologic process. It is the physical activity of sound falling on our ears. Hearing is involuntary and happens without any intended effort. I can sit on the front porch of my home and hear the sound of passing vehicles, of a train in the distance, the sounds of flying insects, fallen leaves rustling in the wind, and a distant bark—all unintentional.

Now, ask yourself a couple of hard questions, "How often have you attended a meeting, a conference, or a group conversation and heard voices and discussions but have not really listened? How often have you witnessed others who were hearing but not actually listening?"

Listening, unlike hearing, is an intentional activity. Listening implies that you are paying attention to the sounds and deriving meaning from them. Listening requires thinking and concentrating to achieve understanding. You may listen to appreciate, you may listen to empathize, you may listen to understand, and you may listen to gain knowledge—all done so intentionally.

Listening requires mental and physical (via body language) exertion. In the next section of this chapter we will explore various techniques to enhance your listening skills.

4.3   SHARPENING YOUR LISTENING SKILLS

What can you do to enhance your listening skills? It starts with intention (i.e., the intention to become a better listener by making every communication richer for all the parties involved). Develop better habits for listening by using the following techniques:

1. **Show intention**—Show your willingness and your intention to listen and understand. You can physically display your intention by focusing your attention on the person talking. Leaning forward displays intention. Use eye contact (avoid staring at people) to display intention. Physically making a note when an important point has been made displays intention. Your facial expressions

can indicate if you are engaged and are listening. Showing your intention encourages openness with the speaker.

2. **Observe**—Observe and look for engagement (or nonengagement). Is the other person engaged in the conversation? Look for those nonverbal cues, such as eye contact, eye movement, and body language. Incorporate those visual things with the things you hear, think, and analyze for understanding.

3. **Ignore distractions**—Do not get distracted or allow yourself to be distracted. Your role, your job in a communication event, is to listen with intent. If you're going to a meeting or to meet someone (regardless of seniority), ignore the distractions. Be fully present. Turn off your phone or place it on *do not disturb* (better to not have a vibrating phone, as that can also be a distraction). Ignore any side chatter or noise. Avoid any visual distractions and focus your visual attention on the speaker.

4. **Paraphrase**—When you paraphrase, you summarize what you heard by using your own words. Paraphrasing raises the awareness that you are listening and that you are confirming what you thought you heard. Paraphrasing saves time and increases understanding. It establishes connection with the speaker. Paraphrasing may also provide the speaker an opportunity to clarify or add additional information.

   If you paraphrase, assume the burden of understanding. For example, it's much better to say, "If I understand you correctly, this is what I took away . . ." as opposed to, "You told us that. . . ." Make the paraphrase a positive experience and consider the speaker's feelings.

   When you paraphrase, you can provide a summary of the facts (as you understand them). You can number or outline your points (i.e., "I took away three key points."). You can provide a contrast of views or different perspectives. Make your paraphrase as effective as possible by making it easy to follow and understand.

5. **Acknowledge feelings**—Acknowledge the feelings or emotions of the speaker. Show empathy and attempt to understand, but don't make hasty judgments or assume the underlying reasons for the emotions. Acknowledge the speaker's feelings but avoid saying, "I know how you feel," because you don't. It is better to say, "I can't blame you for feeling that way. I would be angry, too, if. . . ."

6. **Echo**—Echoing is a simple but effective technique that can be used to clarify what you heard or to obtain additional information. Echo means repeating what you heard using the speaker's own words (usually the tail end of a statement). See the following example of two conversations about the same situation. Conversation One does not employ the echo technique; the second conversation does.

CONVERSATION ONE (NO ECHO)

Interviewer: Thank you for taking the time to meet with me. I understand you are having problems with your existing project portfolio management system.

Client: Yes, I need a new system.

Interviewer: Okay, I see. What features do you need?

Client: I'll send you a list.

CONVERSATION TWO (WITH ECHO)

Interviewer: Thank you for taking the time to meet with me. I understand you are having problems with your existing project portfolio management system.

Client: Yes, I need a new system.

Interviewer: You need a new system?

Client: Yes, I do. The one I'm using now takes too long to update because it is no longer in sync with the accounting system, and we have to manually update the portfolio system.

Interviewer: You have to manually update the portfolio system?

Client: That's right. We changed the accounting system a while back and no one bothered to update the portfolio system.

Interviewer: So, if we update the portfolio system to interface with the accounting system, will that resolve the timing issues?

Client: Yes.

You can see from these simplified examples that the echo technique clarified the client's needs and may have resulted in significant savings (avoiding the replacement of the portfolio system).

To develop this technique, try the following exercise: Call upon a trusted friend, coworker, or mentor and role play an upcoming conversation with your boss, a key executive, or a customer. In your role play, intentionally use the echo technique, and after your role play, perform a debrief with your role-play partner to see what worked or could be improved.

7. **Avoid interrupting**—Always listen with the objective to *understand*. Avoid interrupting the speaker and don't cut off the speaker in order to express your own point of view or thoughts. Do not mentally interrupt your flow of listening. The speaker may say something that triggers a new thought or an opposing point of view, but have the discipline to stay focused on the speaker's message. At the appropriate time, you can paraphrase what you heard or you can ask a clarifying question.

8. **Seek to understand**—By seeking to understand what the speaker is saying, you improve your listening and you may uncover hidden messages. If emotion is used, try to understand what is causing the emotion. If the speaker repeats certain words or phrases, try to understand why. Understand the language of the speaker by paying attention to the speaker's preference for words when making a point or presenting a point of view. For example, a speaker who favors visual motivation tends to use phrases such as, "I see . . ." or "It looks like. . . ." A speaker who favors auditory motivation will use phrases such as, "I hear . . ." or "It sounds like. . . ." A speaker who favors kinesthetic or physical motivation will use phrases such as, "I feel . . ." or "It feels like. . . . "

4.4   UNDERSTANDING THE BARRIERS TO LISTENING EFFECTIVELY

To listen effectively, consider the following common barriers:

1. You may be shaping a response while someone is speaking to make a point. You are not listening. Hold back mentally on your response until after the speaker has completed making their point.

2. Your mind might be wandering while someone else is speaking. People speak at 80 to 120 words a minute, and we can process information (e.g., think, at a much faster rate, 150 to 200 words per minute). With this excess cerebral capacity, our minds tend to wander. Maintain the discipline to focus on the conversation.

3. You stop listening because the topic is of little interest or offensive. Rather than informing the speaker, you disengage through your body language, facial gestures, looking at the time, etc.

4. You stop listening because you don't have the time. Your preference may be to postpone the conversation, but you do not say that to the speaker. You may be concerned that requesting a postponement might initiate a negative response. Consider acknowledging that the conversation is important enough to continue at another time for the benefit of both parties.

5. Over time, attention spans become diminished as we are inundated by distractions (texts, emails, social media, videos, etc.). Microsoft has found that the average attention span since the year 2000 has dropped from 12 to eight seconds. A goldfish has an attention span of nine seconds.[1] A British advertising agency found that, on average, people at home switch from devices (phone, tablet, laptop, TV, etc.) an average of 21 times per hour. This is germane to social media as a distraction. Remind yourself that your focus should be on the conversation.

6. You stop listening because you assume that you know what the other will say. In your mind (or sometimes out loud), you finish the other person's sentence. Consider holding back until the speaker has completed their thought.

7. You make the assumption that you can multitask and, therefore, you can listen while doing something else. Neuroscience explains that this is not true. The brain can do only one thing at a time, but can switch quickly from one mental task to another. Consequently, people cannot listen attentively while doing something else. You need to maintain the discipline of focusing on the conversation and avoid performing other tasks.

8. You stop listening because you don't understand what the other person is telling you. Instead of shutting down, you can ask clarifying questions.

9. You stop listening because you disagree with an opposing view rather than exploring the basis for the opposing view. You may be guilty of *confirmation bias*, where you filter only what you want to hear or what confirms your position or beliefs. Try to maintain an open mind and be aware of your own biases. See the box on the next page for types of biases that can impact how you listen.

TYPES OF BIAS

Note: When you are listening, be aware of the different types of biases that can influence how people code or decode a message. These biases can build up barriers to change:

- **Bias, in general**—Generic bias can occur when people have a predisposition or prejudged outlook on a topic. For example, some people have a bias against those who practice a different religion.
- **Confirmation bias**—People have a belief on a topic (and the topic could be themselves) and tend to seek/accept information that confirms that particular belief while filtering out information that is contrary to a belief they hold. Artificial intelligence embedded in social media can support confirmation bias by tracking the materials that people read (e.g., when you post a *like*, you are automatically provided links to similar information).
- **Anchoring**—This is the propensity to rely on the first piece of information encountered when making decisions. People begin with an implicitly suggested reference point (the "anchor") and make adjustments to it to reach their estimate. For example, the initial price offered during a negotiation sets the standard for the rest of the negotiation, so that prices lower than the initial price seem more reasonable even if they are still higher than the value provided.

---

10. You may redirect the conversation to a topic of more interest, causing the person who was speaking to lose interest or become annoyed or offended.

One not-so-obvious barrier to listening is a distracted focus, such as a concern of having to do something, other priorities, other commitments, or unresolved or uncomfortable conversations, to name a few. Here is an example of how a leader listened then did something.

Gordon Bethune, CEO of Continental Airlines, tells a story about visiting the Continental Airlines offices and maintenance areas at Houston Intercontinental Airport. It was toward the end of the day and he was walking through a maintenance area where an airplane (cost: upwards of $120 million) was going through routine maintenance and would fly the following morning. A mechanic was working on the landing gear when Gordon walked over and asked him, "How is it going?" The mechanic stopped his work, looked up, and said to the CEO, "Mr. Bethune, do you know how much faster I could complete my work if I really wanted to?" Gordon was stunned at this honesty, and he began to truly understand how important this employee was to the company. If the plane was not ready to leave the following morning, passengers would have to be re-accommodated to other airlines, creating a loss of goodwill and many additional expenses. Gordon asked the mechanic to do his best work and what he (Gordon) could do to help him do his job. The mechanic's response was, "Get rid of all the paperwork we have to do that doesn't make any difference except for the people downtown."

The story goes that Gordon came out to the maintenance parking lot and ceremoniously burned a book of cumbersome policies dubbed the *Thou Shalt Not* book. While we are not sure if it was solely the mechanic's comments that precipitated the mini bonfire, this story underscores the importance of listening and following up when you have the ability to make a difference.

Review the barriers in the previous list and ask yourself if you are guilty of some of these actions. Consider these barriers as you participate in future conversations. The more you pay attention to your habits and work to eliminate these barriers, the better you will become as an effective listener.

4.5   ASKING BETTER QUESTIONS

Asking questions can enhance the communication process and relationships. Asking questions:

1. Signals that you are listening and that you seek understanding
2. Promotes conversations versus monologues
3. Tests assumptions (both yours and the speaker's)
4. Helps clarify understanding
5. Helps explore options and keeps dialogue open

Asking better questions is a habit that can be developed. The following tips can help:

1. **Prepare a list of questions prior to the communications event—** Anticipate what questions may need to be asked for the event. Your questions should support the objective of seeking an understanding. Be willing to ask questions that might make you uncomfortable but will lead to a healthier discussion and may advance the relationship. Your questions should also be considerate of the people involved. You will not be conducting an interrogation; you are participating in a conversation.

2. **Use open-ended questions to promote conversations and healthy dialogues**—Have more open-ended questions than closed (yes or no) questions. Use closed questions to clarify.

3. **Use questions to tactfully uncover personal, business, or political agendas**—Plan these questions ahead of time and, if necessary, seek feedback prior to the communications event to ensure that these questions do not derail the event.

4. **Ask your team to help you understand their perspective**—Try to understand their concerns, their frustrations, and their solutions in order to communicate a willingness to listen and move to a solution.

5. **Ask the *why* question**—Asking why can reveal the true motive or agenda. This question can be effective in getting to the root cause of a situation or position. Asking why can reduce unnecessary conversations or added work. One form of a why question is to ask, "Why is this important to you?" The answer may result in a different conversation but will lead to better results. Consider role playing your questions with a friend, peer, or mentor prior to a major or critical communications event.

THE 5 WHYS TECHNIQUE

The *5 Whys Technique*: This technique was developed by Sakichi Toyoda, the founder of Toyota Industries. Simply put, this technique asks "why?" five times in succession to get to the root cause of an issue or problem. Here is a simple example:

Problem: The meeting was ineffective.

- **Why?** We ran out of time to cover all the topics.
- **Why?** Half of the participants arrived 15 minutes late.
- **Why?** They were coming from another building on campus.
- **Why?** They were attending a meeting at the operational facility.
- **Why?** They were attending a mandated weekly operational meeting that does not end until 9:00 a.m.

Possible resolution: Consider a different start time or meeting day.

4.6   FOCUS AREA UPDATE FOR LISTENING AND QUESTIONING

Consider the lessons in this chapter and list your two top focus areas for improvement.

FOCUS AREAS FOR CHAPTER 4

Focus area 1—Describe a behavior that would improve your listening and questioning skills (e.g., I would like to improve my listening skills by not interrupting the other speaker in a conversation):

_____

_____

_____

Focus area 2—Describe a behavior that would minimize the barriers to effective listening (e.g., I want to become more aware of confirmation bias and practice maintaining an open mind):

_____

_____

_____

While you have captured focus areas for this chapter in the space above, we encourage you to go to www.jrosspub.com/CLT where you can download a blank form to keep track of your focus areas created in exercises throughout this book. The template will prove invaluable in your work to prioritize focus areas in Chapters 9, 13, and 14.

4.7   KEY TAKEAWAYS

To summarize the key takeaways in this chapter, let's apply the technique of asking a few questions. Perform your own knowledge check by responding to these questions:

1. Do you understand the benefits of improving your listening and questioning skills?
2. Can you articulate the difference between hearing and listening? Become intentional in your listening. Move from hearing to listening and make it a habit.
3. Can you identify the various methods to enhance your listening skills? Begin intentionally using these techniques to enhance your listening for all of your communication events.
4. Can you identify the various barriers to listening effectively?
5. Are you confident that you can enhance your questioning skills? Begin preparing questions for each critical communications event. Consider role playing an event to *test* your questions.

ENDNOTE

1. McSpadden, Kevin. 2015. "You Now Have a Shorter Attention Span than a Goldfish." *Time.com*. Retrieved October 19, 2021, from https://time.com/3858309/attention-spans-goldfish/.

CHAPTER 5

RECEIVING AND GIVING FEEDBACK—ARE YOU READY?

"We all need people who will give us feedback. That's how we improve."

—Bill Gates

CHAPTER ROADMAP

The purpose of this chapter is to improve in situations where you are *receiving* and *giving* feedback. Both scenarios present an opportunity to learn about yourself and others. Feedback can be almost anything: performance reviews, a raised eyebrow after you make a comment, grades received during your school years, performance at athletic events, comments from parents, coaches, and the list goes on ad infinitum.

Rather than a positive learning experience, feedback about ourselves can seem more like a root canal. However, when people are committed to learning and growing, they really have no choice but to figure out how to mine value from feedback—whether they are prepared to accept it or not—even when that feedback seems wrong, inaccurate, or poorly delivered. Consequently, this chapter's initial focus is on developing habits for benefiting from feedback about yourself. Next, the chapter focuses on to how to give feedback that will have the desired impact. The following list describes a roadmap for your journey through this chapter:

1. Introduction—the concept of feedback
2. Your experiences when receiving feedback
3. Barriers to listening to or learning from feedback
4. A story—the four hot buttons

5. Why people reject feedback about themselves—managing the hot buttons
6. When and how to reject feedback
7. Capturing focus areas for improving how you receive feedback
8. Your experiences when giving feedback
9. Giving feedback is a two-way street
10. How to give impactful feedback
11. Capturing focus areas for improving how you give feedback
12. Prioritize focus areas for receiving and giving feedback
13. Key takeaways from this chapter

5.1   INTRODUCTION

This chapter begins with an assertion that *feedback is essential to grow one's skills/abilities.* Another way to say that is: *growth is a function of feedback and motivation*—as expressed in the equation below:

$$\text{Growth} = \text{Function (Feedback, Motivation)}$$

Motivation is what you supply. This chapter will supply tools and techniques to assist you in mining value from feedback.

The scope of feedback in the equation is broad. It includes verbal feedback from others, your own observations (e.g., body language, observations about your environment, etc.), and learning from your experiences and the experiences of others. That being said, we will focus more on direct forms of feedback that involve conversations where you *receive* and *give* feedback.

Feedback about ourselves, whether requested or volunteered by others, is governed by the communication process where the sender's and receiver's participation is seasoned with their life experiences, personality traits, gender, age, cultural background, biases, etc. Not surprisingly, there is ample opportunity for feedback about ourselves to have unintended consequences, including no consequence at all. In addition, considerable attention has been given regarding how to give feedback, including training on how to conduct performance evaluations at work; feedback about our public speaking skills at Toastmasters; coaching, training, and self-help books and articles; and advice from all kinds of sources. Far less attention has been given on how to receive and benefit from feedback about ourselves. To test this assertion in a qualitative way, we performed an internet search on the subject of feedback. As a result of the search, we looked at over 50 books—only two mentioned *receiving* feedback. The first was *The Art of Giving and Receiving Feedback*[1] and the second was *Thanks for the Feedback: The Art and Science of Receiving Feedback Well.*[2] You may enjoy either book, but we strongly recommend the second one by Douglas Stone and Sheila Heen.

5.2 RECEIVING FEEDBACK ABOUT YOURSELF— YOUR EXPERIENCES

Think about situations where you have received feedback about yourself whether formal (e.g., a performance evaluation at work) or informal, such as a comment from a friend about something you did or said:

1. Was it a good experience in the sense that you learned something about yourself and benefited from the feedback? If so, it was a positive experience.
2. Were there experiences at the other extreme where you did not learn anything and received no benefit? In fact, you may have literally rejected the feedback or were offended by it. If so, it was a negative experience.
3. Were there other experiences between these extremes where you learned something but did not benefit much from the feedback?

Think about these experiences and record no more than two situations where the feedback was meaningful and benefited you in some way. In addition, add comments that underscore and/or support why the feedback benefited you. Before you start, the following list has some tips or *thought starters* that may help you quantify why the experience was meaningful:

1. There were objective measures in place for the feedback. This often is the case in athletic endeavors. A useful acronym when receiving feedback is SBI (specific, behavior, impactful). That is to say, the feedback was *specific* to ensure understanding, *behavior*-based examples were given to ensure desired changes, and the feedback was *impactful* in the sense that an improvement would have a desired outcome. To improve your golf score, the feedback may include situations where you did well. For example, a coach

informs you that your golf score improves (impact) when you keep your attention focused on the ball (behavior) as your body moves through the swing (specific). When projects are over budget in the workplace, feedback can be specific in terms of variance from budget, root causes can be identified, and the impact of changes can be measured over time.

2. You were committed to improving in an area that impacted your job or personal life. An example would include public speaking.
3. You had time to listen and absorb a few key areas where you could focus. Feedback was clear, concise, and not overwhelming.
4. The person giving the feedback was credible.
5. Improvements occurred in a short period of time.

Experience 1—Describe the feedback you received, including why it was meaningful to you (e.g., I was told after a meeting that I argued with people who disagreed with my recommendations and those people disengaged from further discussion. This was meaningful to me because I was unaware I was arguing. I wanted to encourage debate):

_____

_____

_____

List ways in which the feedback you received was beneficial (e.g., I am now more aware of how forceful and direct I can be when making my point. I have modified my approach when presenting recommendations, paraphrasing what people say to assure I understand):

_____

_____

_____

_____

Experience 2—Describe the feedback you received, including why it was meaningful to you:

_____

_____

_____

List ways in which the feedback you received was beneficial:

_____

_____

_____

Now turn the coin over, so to speak, and list no more than two experiences where the feedback was not meaningful, you did not benefit from it, and/or it was stressful/difficult to listen to the messenger. Also, add comments that underscore/support why the feedback did not benefit you.

Here are some thought starters that may help you quantify why the experience did not benefit you:

1. From your perspective, the feedback was false or inaccurate.
2. The person giving the feedback was not credible.
3. The feedback did not focus on the reason you requested the feedback.
4. Too many points were covered. The experience was overwhelming and it was difficult to understand the most important points.
5. The feedback was not timely and the details were lost in your memory bank, especially the feelings that were involved at the time.
6. No opportunity to implement the feedback was given.
7. The feedback was vague or not specific, and you were not sure what it meant (e.g., someone tells you to be more assertive).

8. The feedback included a disconcerting or off-putting label, such as you were late, your reports were incomplete, you are pushy, or you are too laid back. The feedback was focused on you rather than the performance or outcome.

Experience 1—Describe feedback you received, including why it was *not* meaningful to you (e.g., I was told I was too quiet in meetings and appeared that I was not interested in what other people were saying. This feedback was not helpful to me because I felt I was being judged as a person):

_____

_____

_____

List reasons you believe the feedback was of little or no benefit (e.g., the feedback I received was not beneficial because I felt attacked and withdrew from future discussion with the person who gave the feedback. I may have missed opportunities for beneficial feedback based on one experience):

_____

_____

_____

_____

Experience 2—Describe feedback you received, including why it was *not* meaningful to you:

_____

_____

_____

List reasons you believe the feedback was of little or no benefit:

_____

_____

_____

Are there any behaviors that jump out from the preceding analyses? Are there any behaviors you should do more of, less of, start doing, or stop doing? If so, take the opportunity to list no more than two focus areas where you want to change your behavior to improve *your ability to learn from feedback*.

INITIAL FOCUS AREAS: RECEIVING FEEDBACK

Focus area 1—Describe a behavior that would improve how you learn from receiving feedback (e.g., when receiving constructive feedback, I want to focus on finding value in what is said rather than defending my behavior):

_____

_____

Focus area 2—Describe a behavior that would improve how you learn from receiving feedback:

_____

_____

5.3 ENABLERS AND BARRIERS TO FEEDBACK ABOUT OURSELVES

In the previous section you listed focus areas that would provide benefits, whether that feedback is complementary or constructive. Consider these additional points that may help you clarify your focus areas when receiving feedback:

1. Seek feedback early when you are struggling to accomplish a task or result rather than waiting until someone asks you why expectations have not been met.
2. Seek more information when feedback is abstract or not specific. For example, when someone says, "Be more assertive," what do they mean? Ask for examples: how does someone speak more assertively? What situations are being discussed? If a person was more assertive, what result would be achieved?
3. When feedback is emotional (e.g., anger, finger pointing, threatening, etc.), explore the *feelings* rather than debate the words.
4. Prioritize the feedback and agree on the most important points.
5. Allow enough time to have a conversation about the feedback to ensure it is understood. When there is an expectation attached to the feedback, are you committed to fulfilling the expectation? If not, inform the giver that you appreciate the feedback and explain what you *can* do rather than what you *can't* do. This recommendation assumes you have the option to negotiate a commitment.
6. Be aware of the biases (everyone has them) that can impact the motivation of the person providing feedback and also how you interpret it. Biases can build up barriers to change (refer to Chapter 4, Section 4 for more about biases).

Let's now consider barriers to obtaining feedback about ourselves:

1. **The feedback is false**[3]—In this situation, you perceive that the feedback is false (e.g., you are poor in math, you are inconsiderate of others, you are not a team player, you're a reckless driver, etc.). The feedback may not be consistent with the data you have or it is not consistent with your perceptions of reality. In the extreme, it's like someone telling you that $2 + 2 = 5$ when you *know* that $2 + 2 = 3$ (in the world of behavior, where perceptions are reality, absolute truths, such as $2 + 2 = 4$, are unlikely to exist). Consequently, it is likely that the feedback will be refused. Your responses to such feedback may include one or all of the following:
   - You stop listening.
   - You argue the point of truth.

- You become defensive and argumentative.
- You convince yourself the giver of feedback did not understand or misinterpreted the situation.

Whatever the response, it is likely you will stop listening and reject the feedback. Can you learn from feedback that you consider to be false? The answer is *yes* (if you try):

- Consider whether all aspects of the feedback are false. Rather than closing off, are there diamonds in the rough? Take a breath, slow down, and ask yourself whether there is something to learn, even though you feel the feedback for the most part is false. You may have blind spots that include a lack of awareness about a specific area of your behavior or personality but are known or visible to others. Those blind spots may lead you to refuse feedback that others see as barriers to your effectiveness as a communicator and leader. (More on blind spots in Appendix A, the Johari Window.)
- Consider the opportunity to explore how the person providing feedback developed the perception. What was the basis of his/her feedback? Why is the feedback telling you 2 + 2 = 5? Focus not on the validity of the feedback but the underlying cause of the perception. Decide whether there is learning or insight on how to prevent such perceptions in the future. Use the active listening techniques from Chapter 4 to determine how the perception was developed and decide what, if any, behaviors you want to change.

2. **You perceive that the feedback is not valid**—It may seem that *false* and *not valid* mean the same thing. The difference is subtle. For purposes of this book, false has to do with the accuracy of feedback (e.g., close to the truth). Validity has to do with the credibility of the feedback. People may feel feedback is invalid because:

- The person giving the feedback is not a credible source of information and that perception impacts our ability to listen and learn from the feedback. This is often the case where a personal relationship exists with the provider of the feedback. In these situations, the receiver focuses on the person giving the feedback rather than the content of the feedback.[4] For example, we all probably know people who attempt to finish a sentence for us because they know us well. That assumption often gives people the *license* to offer feedback in areas where we feel they lack credibility. Think about situations where you have received feedback from a significant other. Have there been emotionally charged conversations? Often the language in such feedback is charged with emotion because we want to be accepted rather than criticized by someone who is important to us. Consider experiences where you have received feedback from a person with whom you have a relationship/history. Can we learn from this source of feedback? The answer is *yes* and here's how:

- Focus on the content of the feedback rather than the person providing the feedback and be open to the content. Ask yourself, "Is there something to learn in the content of the feedback?"

- Use listening techniques to explore the *feelings* behind the feedback, particularly when emotional levels are rising. You don't have to agree or accept the feedback, but you may need to *own* why the person is providing the feedback. Ask yourself, "How did I contribute to the feedback and what behaviors do I own?" Then decide whether there are behaviors you want to change.

3. **The feedback is inconsistent with your self-image**—There is another area where feedback about ourselves may sometimes fall into a *black hole* of learning. All of us have a concept of ourselves concerning who we are, our values, and our perception of our reality; ideas that have been ingrained in our psyche throughout our years of learning from our successes and failures. People invest a lot of time and energy into building this self-image. Feedback that is not consistent with this *self* can be threatening or at least disconcerting. Stone and Heen call this barrier *identity*.[5] Whether the feedback is false or offered by someone who does not have credibility is another matter. This feedback may jeopardize a person's perception of themselves as an individual. They may reject the feedback, but it is just as likely that they will internalize this feedback and allow it to weaken their foundation. They may become like a deer in the headlights, so to speak. The stress may impact a person's confidence, cause them to withdraw, or impact them in other negative or unsettling ways. How can you work with, manage, and learn from feedback that threatens your self-concept?

- Recognize the threat, take a breath, and manage the emotional reaction. Use self-talks to remind yourself to be who *you* really are (everyone else is already taken).
- Rather than react, defend, go on the offensive, or withdraw, transition to *exploratory mode*. For example, "tell me more."
- Use active listening techniques such as echoing in order to explore feelings, emotions, and the behaviors that caused the feedback, rather than reacting emotionally to the feedback. Build up the habit of asking for more information, clarification, and examples.
- Be aware of overreacting by asking yourself, "Is this feedback relevant in all situations? Do I do this all the time? What is the feedback about and what is it not about?"

4. **You ask the *wrong* person for feedback**—The person you requested the feedback from is biased in some way or does not want to give objective feedback that outlines areas for improvement, believing that the *perceived* criticism will harm your relationship. Seek feedback from people whom you trust to be accurate and objective. While people may prefer friendly feedback, accurate feedback is more valuable.

5.4   NOT ALL FEEDBACK HAS THE SAME PURPOSE

The purpose of most feedback is to create action. However, feedback can come in different contexts as shown here:[6]

1. **Coaching**—The person is asking for ways to improve or grow
2. **Evaluation**—The person wants to know how they are doing relative to expectations
3. **Approval**—The person seeks recognition, wanting to be recognized as a person who matters

When you seek one kind of feedback, such as coaching or approval for example, and get an evaluation, it is like ships passing in the night—unaware of each other! When the person providing feedback and the person receiving feedback are not aligned on the purpose of the feedback, the opportunity for learning may be missed. The person providing feedback may feel any of the following:

1. The receiver is not interested in learning or growing

2. The receiver is rejecting feedback when they should appreciate the feedback that the provider feels is important
3. The provider may develop an unfavorable bias in future observations of the receiver's performance
4. The provider may feel the receiver does not respect or appreciate their credibility

The person receiving the feedback may feel:

1. The provider is rambling and not listening to the request for a specific type of feedback
2. The provider is insensitive to the receiver's need to obtain information to help improve performance
3. The receiver may be reluctant to seek feedback in the future
4. The provider does not appreciate the receiver's commitment to develop and grow

---

FEEDBACK—NOT WHAT I EXPECTED

Barbara (speaking to Fred about her conversation with her supervisor, Bob): Gosh, I stopped Bob in the hall after the presentation this morning and asked him how he thought it went. We got approval for funding of our project. Everyone commented that my presentation was really good, but the conversation morphed into feedback about the report that I gave Bob at the end of last quarter.

Fred: Sounds like it was not a good experience.

Barbara: No, I was looking for a *pat on the back*, and instead, I got an evaluation of something I did last quarter. His feedback took twenty minutes!

To overcome these missteps, it is incumbent on the receiver to signal the provider as to the type of feedback being requested. For example, when preparing for the feedback conversation, the receiver can inform the provider the type of feedback they are requesting by offering guidance:[7]

1. Ask what you can start doing, stop doing, and do more of.
2. Ask about your strengths—what skills are most valuable?
3. Blind spots—what behaviors are holding you back? If you were to change one thing, what would that be?
4. Situation—in what situations does the provider see you making the greatest impact? When has the provider seen you struggle or be less effective?

Suppose the provider diverts the conversation away from the requested type of feedback. In that case, the receiver can recognize what the provider is saying, express appreciation, then redirect the conversation and give examples of the type of feedback being requested. In this instance it is important that the receiver recognize that the provider had additional comments for feedback and offer an opportunity for the provider to give the feedback they felt was important.

The following story of Ann and John provides a real-life example of how conversations involving feedback can go way off track, but then re-align to provide a learning experience. Think about situations that you have experienced where the dynamic and the outcome were similar to what you read in this story. Consider whether there are key takeaways for you in Part 2 of the story.

PART 1: FEEDBACK GONE WRONG

John considers himself a very good driver. In college, 35 years ago, he damaged his car in a rainstorm. Since then, he has not had another accident, no speeding tickets, and only a few parking tickets on his rap sheet. In the year 2000, John started road racing (on tracks with multiple turns, elevation changes, etc.) and advanced to the point where he coached beginner through advanced sports car racing enthusiasts, highway patrol officers, teenagers in driving schools, and performance driving by appointment in all types of cars (e.g., Ferrari, Porsche, McLaren, Matias, BMW, Lamborghini, etc.). The data supports John's image of himself as a competent driver.

Ann, John's wife, has been in several fender benders over the years and has an assortment of tickets. Four years ago, as a passenger in a car, she was injured in a collision, breaking her sternum and several ribs. Painful! John and Ann witnessed a fatal accident in 2016, but in no way were involved. Ann has become fearful and alert in situations where she feels at risk in a car. *The stage is set.*

John is driving on a road with one lane in each direction. He is approaching an intersection with a traffic signal that is red in his direction. As he gets closer to the intersection, it changes to green. The oncoming lane is gridlocked and blocked, but John's lane is open with the green light. Cars are approaching the intersection to John's right, but they now have a red light. He is about to enter the intersection when he sees a car nearing the intersection from his right side. He sees the car slowing in his peripheral vision, and John drives through the intersection. In a debrief for this book, John testifies that he saw the nose of the approaching

(continues)

car go down, meaning the driver was on the brakes. He was also looking in John's direction. He was going to stop (apparently, race car drivers can process all this information in microseconds!). As John drives through the intersection, Ann screams, "That car is going to hit us!"

Ann: Oh my God!

John: What?

Ann: Didn't you see that car? That car back there almost hit us!

John: I saw the car. It wasn't going to hit us. I had a green light.

Ann: You don't have to race. You are not on a racetrack! You are so *reckless*!

John: I am not reckless. I saw the nose of the car go down. He was going to stop.

Ann: Nose? What nose? Cars don't have noses. A front and back, a top and bottom.

John: (defensively) Look, we were okay. We did not have an accident. You're *overreacting*.

Ann: You are reckless.

For the rest of the trip home, the silence was deafening.

As we look at the interaction from John's perspective, Ann punched all four *hot buttons*:

1. **False**—We did not have an accident, and we were not in danger. John believes he is not reckless.
2. **Invalid feedback**—Ann is not qualified to critique John's driving.
3. **Self-concept**—I am not reckless. I am a competent, experienced driver.
4. **Wrong person**—Ann did not give objective feedback or areas for improvement.

What can we learn from this interaction? John and Ann look at the situation and see it through the lens of their individual life experiences. John is a seasoned driver with years of training and experience driving confidently in stressful situations. Ann has had injuries in an accident and was emotionally impacted by a fatal accident. They interpret the situation against those experiences. Ann is fearful and John is comfortable and confident. Ann imagines a possible accident. John sees normal driving. Ann labels John reckless. John labels Ann as histrionic.

Let's now go to Part 2 of the story about John and Ann.

PART 2: RECEIVING FEEDBACK THE RIGHT WAY

A few days after the conversation in the car between John and Ann, John is laboring to understand how that interaction went so poorly. He begins to realize that he was reacting to who was speaking to him and the label *reckless* rather than the emotion that Ann was expressing—*fear*. John stated that he reacted to what he heard—the word *reckless*—rather than how Ann was feeling. John felt that Ann could have been clearer in expressing her fear, but he also realized he had contributed to the breakdown in communication by his emotional response. John is now feeling rather good that he has a better understanding of what happened and wants to avoid circumstances like that in the future. At this point, he is looking for approval from Ann: recognition for coming to talk to her about it and working on managing situations in the future. Again, *the stage is set*.

John: I have been thinking about what happened when we were driving the other day and how that conversation escalated to where we were both upset. It occurred to me that I did not recognize that you were afraid. My driving scared you, and you may have been reacting to that fear. I reacted to how I was feeling and not how you were feeling. I felt criticized.

Ann: (interrupting John mid-sentence) And you don't like to be criticized!

John: (after a long pause) I was not expecting that reaction.

Ann: (after a long pause) Ouch! That hurts, huh? Did I just break your bubble?

John: Maybe not, but I didn't expect that comment. I was looking for how we can avoid having a similar situation in the future.

John and Ann got back on track after this dialogue and worked on ways to manage situations where Ann feels at risk while John is driving. John committed to be more aware of situations where Ann would feel at risk and practice avoiding those situations.

What happened in Part 2 of this conversation?

1. John was seeking acknowledgment and recognition, but got an evaluation instead.
2. John felt he was being told he was *always* reckless (a distortion).
3. John did not explore what Ann was feeling and address her feelings (not in the middle of the intersection but soon afterward).
4. Ann reacted to her fear by blaming John.

5. Ann did not recognize John's driving ability but rather *condemned* him for putting them at risk.

While it would have been inappropriate in the middle of the intersection to express appreciation for John's ability, that recognition could have come moments later, followed by a request to avoid those situations in the future.

We can envision a happy ending to the John and Ann driving conundrum. However, when Ann deviated from John's expectations in Part 2, there was an opportunity for more learning from Ann's comment about John not liking criticism. John could go back to that comment and ask Ann for more information:

1. Tell me more about what you mean when you say, "I don't like criticism."
2. When does that happen? How do I react?
3. What are the circumstances?
4. When you tell me that *I don't like criticism*, it makes me feel like I never accept feedback; is that what you mean?

The point here is to listen and go back and clarify/explore components of feedback you receive about yourself.

5.5   HOW TO MANAGE OR DECLINE FEEDBACK

Although we have concentrated on learning from feedback in this chapter, you actually do have a choice whether to accept it. You can *graciously* decline feedback.

Before we discuss situations where you may want to manage or decline feedback, we feel we must remind you about your responsibility to clarify the type of feedback that you are requesting. That is to say, the following list *excludes* situations where you have requested one type of feedback—for example, you request coaching and you receive an evaluation. In this circumstance, thank the provider for the feedback and redirect the conversation to the kind of feedback you are requesting. Here are three situations to consider when you may not accept feedback:[8]

1. **Time**—This is a situation where you are limited in time; not sure you want to accept the feedback, but will consider it later. This is often the case when the feedback was unsolicited, you were not

expecting it, and you are not sure you want to accept it. You need time to think about the feedback and whether you want to act on it. How can you manage these situations?

- Acknowledge the feedback
- State clearly you need time to consider the feedback
- Consider the feedback and let the person providing the feedback know your decision
- Thank the provider for their comments and indicate that aspects of the feedback were relevant and that you will take their feedback as a learning experience in future circumstances

2. **Thanks, but no thanks**—There may be situations where you do not accept the recommendations housed in the feedback. Often this happens when one person tells another person, "This is how I would handle the situation." (The person is suggesting you should be like them.) What can you do in a situation where it is clear that you will not accept recommendations that are housed in the feedback?

- Acknowledge the feedback (e.g., "So, you are saying . . .") by clearly indicating or stating that you have a different perception of the situation and that, consequently, you are comfortable with your behavior.
- Be firm but polite because you may want to leave the door open for people to provide feedback in the future that may be valuable.

3. **It's not a *no*, but a *hell no***—This type of feedback is characterized by abusive language, threats, personal attacks, and continual criticism over a period of time. In these situations, avoid *fighting fire with fire*. Rather, be firm, honest, and focus on how the feedback is making you feel and not whether the feedback is accurate. Tell the person providing the feedback to *stop*. If the feedback continues, however, you have several options:

- Walk away from the conversation
- Walk away from the relationship if the feedback continues
- Take the situation to a senior manager or the human resource department if the situation occurs in your work environment

Do you have additional insights about receiving feedback from the material in Sections 5.3 (*Enablers and Barriers to Feedback About*

Ourselves), 5.4 (*Not All Feedback Has the Same Purpose*), or 5.5 (*How to Manage or Decline Feedback*)? If so, take the opportunity to update your focus areas about receiving feedback.

FINAL FOCUS AREAS: RECEIVING FEEDBACK

Focus area 1—Describe a behavior that would improve how you learn from receiving feedback (e.g., when I believe feedback I have received is not true, I will ask questions to find out how the person giving the feedback formed their opinion to determine whether my behavior is causing misperceptions):

_____

_____

_____

Focus area 2—Describe a behavior that would improve how you learn from receiving feedback:

_____

_____

_____

5.6 GIVING FEEDBACK—YOUR EXPERIENCES

Up to this point in Chapter 5, the focus has been on *receiving* feedback. The emphasis now shifts to *giving* feedback that is impactful (e.g., behavior changes, relationship improvements, results/performance improvements, etc.). Consequently, a key assumption when giving feedback is that we expect someone to do something, such as change behavior, reinforce existing behavior so that it continues, or stop doing a behavior that is not effective or offensive. When working with people, we (the authors) have heard them say, "Well, I just wanted people to be aware." Our response has been, "And if they are aware, what do you expect them to do?" Most often, there is an expectation.

As with previous sections of this book, this section starts with the empirical approach to learning from your observations and experience. Describe two experiences when you provided feedback—in either your personal or work life—that was meaningful to you and had an impact on the person receiving it, such as:

1. Positive behavioral changes
2. The feedback was well received
3. There was a dialogue and give-and-take conversation, not just one-way
4. You felt you were understood

Experience 1—Describe a situation where the feedback you gave was impactful (e.g., circumstances, timing of the feedback relative to the event that caused you to give feedback, willingness of the person to receive the feedback, etc.):

_____

_____

_____

What did you do and/or what did the person receiving the feedback do to contribute to the meaningful experience (e.g., you both listened actively, confirmed understanding, clarified purpose, took time to have a conversation, etc.)?

_____

_____

_____

Experience 2—Describe a situation where the feedback you gave was impactful (e.g., circumstances, timing of the feedback relative to the event that caused you to give feedback, willingness of the person to receive the feedback, etc.):

_____

_____

_____

What did you do and/or what did the person receiving the feedback do to contribute to the meaningful experience (e.g., you both listened actively, confirmed understanding, clarified purpose, took time to have a conversation, etc.)?

_____

_____

_____

Now describe two experiences when you provided feedback—in your personal or work life—that were not meaningful or impactful, such as:

1. No behavioral change
2. The feedback was rejected
3. There was a defensive reaction without a meaningful dialogue to clarify understanding
4. You felt you were not understood

Experience 1—Describe a situation where the feedback you gave was not impactful (e.g., circumstances, poor timing of the feedback relative to the event that caused you to give feedback, willingness of the person to receive the feedback, etc.):

_____

_____

_____

What did you do and/or what did the person receiving the feedback do to contribute to the experience (e.g., lack of listening because focus was on responding, did not explore to clarify understanding, the receiver was preoccupied, etc.)?

_____

_____

_____

Experience 2—Describe a situation where the feedback you gave was not impactful (e.g., circumstances, poor timing of the feedback relative to the event that caused you to give feedback, willingness of the person to receive the feedback, etc.):

_____

_____

_____

What did you do and/or what did the person receiving the feedback do to contribute to the experience (e.g., lack of listening because focus was on responding, did not explore to clarify understanding, the receiver was preoccupied, etc.)?

_____

_____

_____

From your experience giving feedback, do certain behaviors stand out? Behaviors you should do more of, less of, start doing, or stop doing? If so, take the opportunity to list no more than two focus areas where you want to change your behavior to improve your ability to give impactful feedback.

INITIAL FOCUS AREAS: GIVING FEEDBACK

Focus area 1—Describe a behavior that would improve how you provide impactful feedback (e.g., when giving feedback, give specific examples and ask questions to ensure the person understands the feedback. Then confirm the feedback is understood):

_____

_____

_____

(continues)

> **Focus area 2**—Describe a behavior that would improve how you provide impactful feedback:
>
> _____
>
> _____
>
> _____

5.7 PRACTICAL GUIDE FOR PROVIDING FEEDBACK

There are several fundamental concepts that apply to providing feedback, including:

1. **Provide SMART feedback**—Where SMART is the acronym for specific, measurable, attainable/achievable, relevant/realistic, time-bound:

   - **Specific**—Feedback should be specific to ensure that it is understood. If someone were to give feedback by saying _be more assertive_, that is not specific, and therefore, is not helpful. More specific information could include:
     - Describe what being more assertive sounds like.
     - Describe how someone would know they were more assertive.
     - Describe circumstances where someone should be more assertive.
     - List benefits of being more assertive.
     - Provide specific examples of situations where the receiver was not assertive along with the consequences that resulted. Give examples of how the situation could have been handled by being more assertive.
     - Check whether the receiver now understands what the giver meant by being more assertive.
   - **Measurable**—There is an intended outcome that can be quantified. How would the receiver know they were being more assertive? In some situations the measures can be

specific and understood (e.g., completing work on time). When the feedback is more abstract, such as, "I want you to exceed my expectations," it will be necessary to give examples and provide more frequent feedback to ensure understanding and align perceptions. When the desired outcome of a behavior cannot be measured, even qualitatively, consider whether the feedback can be impactful and worth giving, or research ways to make the behavior measurable.

- **Attainable/achievable**—Assuming that feedback is given to change behavior, reinforce existing behaviors, etc., then the feedback should have an expected outcome that is attainable, given the receiver's current social, economic, or cultural resources and time availability. When there is a question as to whether the behavior is attainable, consider adjusting the feedback to ensure that expectations can be achieved.

- **Relevant/realistic**—The feedback must be relevant to the receiver, such as improving performance at work, or meaningful to the receiver in the sense of improving relationships, achieving a life goal, etc. "What's in it for the receiver?" That question is the acid test for relevant feedback. If the feedback has an outcome that is important to the provider but not to the receiver, the receiver may comply, but it is unlikely that the receiver will be committed.

- **Time-bound**—After confirming that the feedback is understood and accepted, it is important to confirm a commitment by agreeing on a date or time frame to achieve the desired outcome. Conversations about timing are also helpful in understanding priorities and confirming that the outcome is realistic and achievable. While the provider of the feedback may feel that the feedback has a high priority, the receiver may have other work and personal life priorities that take precedence. Perhaps the best they can do in the current time frame is to recognize and appreciate the feedback, but not commit to any specific outcomes at this point in time.

GIVING FEEDBACK

When providing feedback, be aware of expecting the receiver of the feedback to behave the same way in which the provider does. In the example of giving feedback to someone to be more assertive, that feedback is not relevant to someone whose style is less assertive but is nonetheless effective in achieving desired outcomes. Realize that different behaviors can achieve acceptable outcomes.

---

2. **Feedback involves a conversation**—Feedback is a two-way street between the provider and the receiver. The conversation helps to ensure that:
   - The receiver *understands* the feedback—not just the words but also the feelings behind the words and the cultural context, so that differences in cultural norms do not mask understanding.
   - There is complete alignment on expectations.
   - There is urgency/legitimacy in order to align the priorities.
   - The expectation is understood and a commitment is made.
   - Both the provider and receiver learn from the experience. The provider learns more effective ways to give feedback, and the receiver learns how to receive feedback and how to accept or decline it.
   - There is a willingness to have two-way conversations, which can reduce barriers to accepting feedback.
   - The feedback focuses on behaviors, impact, and outcomes rather than the person or their character, which makes it less likely that the person who is receiving the feedback will feel attacked. Therefore, it is more likely that the person receiving the feedback will listen and at least understand the feedback and the potential benefits.
3. **Self-assessment**—Before *jumping* right into providing feedback, a good practice in almost all situations (perhaps emergency situations are an exception) is to ask the person who is receiving feedback for their perception, their viewpoint, and their assessment of their own behavior/outcomes/performance regarding the focus of the feedback:
   - How do they perceive their behaviors, results achieved, and impact on others?

- Ask them their strengths and areas for improvement.
- What can they do better, continue doing, start doing, or stop doing?
- Ask them to list their goals and what is in the way of achieving those goals. Help them identify ways of overcoming the barriers that are keeping them from achieving their goals rather than telling them what they should do.

5.8 THREE MODES OF FEEDBACK

When feedback is given to someone, it can be any one of three types:

1. **Solicited**—Providing feedback because a person has requested it.
2. **Unsolicited**—Providing feedback that was not requested. It could be a spontaneous response that was the result of observed behavior that has had an impact, either positive or negative, on you or others.
3. **Scheduled feedback**—An example in our work life is a performance appraisal, which compares performance against an expectation. This feedback is more formal. It is usually expected by both the provider and receiver of the feedback.

The amount of feedback given, the time preparing, and the time to follow up depends on the criticality, significance, and perceived impact of the feedback. When you give feedback, consider the continuum shown in Figure 5.1.

Figure 5.1 Feedback criticality continuum

As the provider and/or receiver of feedback move from the left of this continuum to the right, the amount of time in planning, follow-up, importance of understanding, and agreement on expected outcomes increases. It is important that the provider and receiver align on where they are on this continuum. For example, consider a situation where the receiver perceives that the feedback is not critical and that there is a low expectation of change, yet the provider sees the feedback as significant and meaningful. This misalignment can lead to confusion, frustration, and in a work situation, can lead to a poor performance evaluation.

The following list provides more information on the three modes of feedback:

1. **Solicited feedback**—Someone has asked for feedback regarding their own behavior, performance, outcomes, or how to manage a specific situation that is challenging for them.[9] This situation can occur when a friend asks for help with building relationships or with a coaching/mentoring relationship at work. If you receive a request to provide feedback, you must then decide whether to accept. If you decline, a best practice is to provide a reason, such as your lack of qualifications, lack of information to provide accurate feedback, or lack of time for a meaningful conversation for feedback and follow-up. If you decide to give feedback:
   - Before providing feedback, clarify what type of feedback is being requested:
     - *Approval*—The person is looking for recognition (e.g., they are making a contribution).
     - *Coaching*—The person realizes skill deficiencies and is seeking advice or information on how to improve behavior/performance in particular situations.
     - *Evaluation*—The person wants to know how they are doing relative to expectations.
   - Practice active listening (Chapter 4). Ask the receiver their perspective, their opinion, and their feelings about the situation. Getting them involved in the feedback informs you of the type of feedback they are requesting.
   - Confirm with the receiver of the feedback that you understand the purpose of the feedback, the outcomes that are expected, and the importance of the feedback to them (i.e., is it casual or a high priority).

An approach that complements the SMART technique for giving feedback, particularly when the feedback entails changing, is the SBI model. Be *specific* while addressing the *behavior*, not the person, and recognize the *impact* of the existing behavior and how changes could result in different outcomes. Depending on the relationship and the criticality of the feedback, you can clarify the expectation by confirming:

- What does the receiver expect as a result of the feedback? What outcome?
- Is the receiver committed? Explore what they mean when they say they are committed to a specific behavior or result.
- How will the receiver measure progress? What are the success measurements, including time frame?
- What permissions will you be given when commitments are achieved—or not achieved?

When giving solicited feedback, be clear as to whether you intend to provide continual coaching and follow-up sessions. Your time commitment depends on the criticality of the feedback along with the relationship between you and the receiver of the feedback. Actions that are appropriate for a coaching relationship may not be practical for a situation with a personal friend who has asked for feedback on certain behaviors with his children.

2. **Unsolicited feedback**—Someone is volunteering feedback that has not been specifically requested. This feedback can be incidental. For example, you see a neighbor pick up discarded trash and deposit it in a trash can. As you pass by you recognize and express appreciation for the effort. The situation changes when you are compelled to provide feedback that is constructive, offers improvements, or suggests changes. In this situation, the provider cannot assume that the receiver will welcome the feedback or be open to it. The receiver may well resent the feedback. The unintended consequences could include a change in relationship, emotional responses, arguments, and blocks to future communications. The following is a list of guidelines for providing unsolicited feedback:

    - Request permission to provide feedback. For example:
        - May I give you feedback about your responses to Tom during this morning's meeting?

- ◦ May I give you some feedback about the outcomes from the neighborhood meeting?
- ◦ I noticed some people resisted your suggestions during the neighborhood association meeting. May I share my observations with you?
- ◦ I was impressed with how you handled the conflict between Mary and John. May I share my observations with you?

  Use the answers to these questions to assess whether the person is open to feedback at that point in time, or maybe at a later date. The openness to feedback will, to a large extent, depend on the relationship of the parties involved.
- When you are emotional about a circumstance and liable to move from being candid to aggressive, it may be appropriate to take a time out before providing feedback. In that situation, however, remember that as time passes, the relevancy and impact of the feedback decreases.
- What's in it for the receiver? What benefit will the receiver get by listening and changing? The provider can reframe the feedback or forgo giving the feedback when there is no significant benefit for the receiver.
- Determine what you expect as a giver of the unsolicited feedback. If you are expecting a change in behavior and the instance is on the left side of the feedback criticality continuum for the receiver, are your expectations reasonable? If not, you can forgo giving feedback or reframe the feedback so it is impactful to the receiver.
- When the receiver indicates now is not the time, due to a stressful situation or other priorities, suggest an alternative time that would be convenient to have a conversation.

When you do give unsolicited feedback, and you and the receiver are aligned on the criticality of the feedback:

- Clarify what you expect. See Chapter 7, *Consequential Communication*.
- Listen and pay attention to body language, tone, and eye contact for signs that the receiver understands the meaning and feelings behind the words.
- Remember, feedback is a two-way conversation, not a one-way street. Expect the receiver to be engaged, and if they are not, probe as to why.

- Ask if you are understood and what it means to the receiver. Ask the receiver to paraphrase what the feedback meant to them.
- Whether or not the receiver accepts the feedback, express appreciation for their time and attention.

When you are giving unsolicited feedback because the receiver's behavior is affecting you in a negative way, you may have to inform the receiver about the consequences of ignoring the feedback, such as withdrawing from the relationship. In a work environment you may not have the option of withdrawing from the relationship. You may need to escalate the situation, which is the extreme case but not uncommon. Keep in mind that escalation may have unintended consequences for you and the receiver of the feedback.

3. **Formal feedback**—Formal feedback is most frequently given in the workplace, for example, during a performance review. Most organizations have policies about performance reviews and specific time intervals, such as annual, semiannual, etc. It is a good idea that the provider of feedback separates the performance review from salary adjustments so the focus on the performance and how to improve it rather than on the consequences (i.e., getting a raise or getting fired). In theory, this separation is supposed to keep the receiver open-minded about the feedback and focused on improving their work rather than protecting their salary. People tend to make a connection between a performance review and their salary, and therefore, can resist feedback about their performance. Nonetheless, it is important that the provider of the feedback focuses on performance and desired outcomes, offers support where appropriate, and explains the benefits of improved performance or the consequences of not responding to the feedback. Start with the assumption that people want to improve their performance and that the feedback is a positive experience rather than a painful one. While we have discussed many of the upcoming points in other sections, we risk repetition for the sake of clarity and reinforcement of key concepts:
   - Start by asking the receiver of the feedback to self-assess. Direct the conversation toward outcomes, results, performance execution, and enablers, such as relationships. Ask

what they could do differently in the specific situation that they bring up.

- Focus on the strengths of the receiver and a limited number of opportunities for improvement. We recommend suggesting no more than three areas for improvement as a guideline.
- Prepare and be ready with SMART feedback. Evaluating accurately is more important than being kind, friendly, or giving compliments. Of course, giving accurate compliments is a good thing.
- Feedback about job performance should be expressed often, regardless of organizational guidelines (i.e., annual performance appraisals). Giving feedback often allows the provider to *learn* how to provide feedback, how to prepare, how much detail to include, what to highlight, and how to recognize the receiver's blind spots. Short, informal feedback sessions will generate information for the more formal feedback sessions. In addition, informal feedback should be given without delay. That is to say, soon after the event, behavior, or circumstance that warrants feedback. We are not suggesting giving feedback every day, but there should be no surprises during formal feedback sessions—on the positive side or on areas for improvement.

Additional benefits of giving feedback often include:

- Helping the giver of feedback establish openness and transparency. Remember, it's a two-way conversation.
- Uncovering sensitive areas that the receiver has and learning how to manage feedback around those sensitive areas.
- Staying focused in these *informal* feedback conversations. When you provide feedback on the consequences of behaviors, whether to reinforce or offer improvement, remember to comment on any progress that was made in the next session. Look for opportunities to reinforce what was said in the previous feedback session. Avoid bringing up a number of new topics. Rather, look for opportunities to reinforce feedback from previous feedback sessions, particularly where improvements are evident.

5.9   CHALLENGING PERFORMANCE EVALUATIONS

Sooner or later, all of us will be in a situation where, during a review situation, conversations about performance will spiral downward (e.g., resistance, it's not my fault, I didn't have time, it's your fault, etc.). These conversations can have significant consequences. Chapter 7, *Consequential Communications*, elaborates on the subject and offers guidelines. We will not cover that material here but will continue in the genre of giving feedback.

First of all, you can forecast a difficult performance review conversation from previous informal or spontaneous feedback conversations, which is another reason to provide feedback often.

The following conversation is an example of a performance review that took place between JoAnn, the vice president of sales for a large industrial supply distributor, and Percy, the top salesperson. JoAnn has requested this interim review to discuss the fact that Percy is not filing sales call reports on his 10 accounts. The reports are two to four months behind schedule, or they are never filed. This fact has been brought up in one formal performance review and two shorter feedback sessions. The meeting takes place in JoAnn's office.

DIFFICULT PERFORMANCE REVIEWS, PART 1

JoAnn: Hello, Percy. Please have a seat (JoAnn is sitting beside Percy, not behind her desk). How is your father doing?

Percy: He's fine. Wasn't a heart attack, after all. He is going to be on meds for quite a while.

JoAnn: Good to hear.

Percy: (After a pause from JoAnn) I assume you're going to get on my case again about the sales call reports.

JoAnn: Do I need to get on your case, Percy?

Percy: Well, that's all we ever talk about!

JoAnn: Really? That's all we talk about?

Percy: Seems that way to me.

(continues)

JoAnn: I recall last week giving you a shout-out for closing the large Chevron order. And you had 70% participation among your clients in the Habitat for Humanity campaign. I believe you were congratulated on that.

Percy: (Looking a bit sullen) Look, JoAnn, do you want me out selling or in the office filling out paperwork?

JoAnn: The organization needs both. We have talked about this. It's not either/or. It's both.

Percy: I am your top salesman; make a choice—sales or paperwork.

JoAnn: The organization needs both. There are six other salespeople on the team. They get their sales call reports in on time and the quality is good with some minor exceptions.

Percy: But I am the sales leader.

JoAnn: You are. I know that, all the other salespeople and the rest of the organization knows that and appreciates it. All of the salespeople reach their targets except Jacob, and he is improving. Percy, the organization needs both.

Percy: Tell you what; give me Jacob's accounts and let him do the paperwork.

JoAnn: Not an option. We need to grow our younger salespeople. Last week, you left to check on your father's health. While you were gone, people from Lyondell called about an order. The rest of the salespeople stepped up to help out, but we couldn't find anything in the account records or your sales call reports detailing your discussion with Lyondell—commitments made, course of action, or what Lyondell was expecting. It was a scramble. But we kept *your* client satisfied and met their needs. That situation is one example of why the sales call reports are important. I want to stop this back-and-forth over the sales call reports. What can you do to get the sales call reports in on time? It's not what I can do; it's not what Jacob can do; it's what you can do.

Percy: (Annoyed) Okay, if paperwork is so important, take some accounts away, and instead of selling, I'll do all the important paperwork.

JoAnn: Is that what you really want to do?

Percy: No, that's what you want me to do.

After a brief pause the conversation continues.

DIFFICULT PERFORMANCE REVIEWS, PART 2

JoAnn: Percy, I am not going to own this. It's your decision.

Percy: I don't know what to do.

JoAnn: You brought up taking over Jacob's account.

Percy: I wasn't serious. I knew you wouldn't do that.

JoAnn: Okay, I'll offer you a deal. Jacob does a good job on his sales call reports. He needs a mentor to shorten his learning curve as a salesperson, and he really respects you. You work with Jacob—coaching, going on sales calls with him, and taking him on your sales calls to your customers. In exchange, you get him to help you with sales call reports. Learn how he gets his reports done quickly and effectively.

Percy: Are you serious?

JoAnn: Yes, but here's the deal. You go to Jacob and make the arrangement. Be clear on outcomes for both of you. Then both of you explain the arrangement to me. Deal?

Percy: Deal!

JoAnn: So you know my expectations, and I believe I have your commitment for on-time high-quality sales reports and Jacob meets his sales targets within six months. Correct?

Percy: Yes.

JoAnn: What permissions do you give me if your sales reports are not timely or not of acceptable quality?

We stop this case at this point. This was a real-world situation, but there was some paraphrasing.

5.9.1 Key Learnings

1. JoAnn moved from her position (Position A) and Percy's position (B) to a new position (C), involving Jacob.
2. JoAnn used a technique we call a broken record. She kept repeating that the organization needed sales call reports and gave an example of why and how it helped Percy.
3. JoAnn did not accept the *sales or paperwork* offer and was clear about what was needed from Percy.
4. JoAnn answered Percy's comments and gave him appropriate, positive feedback.

5. JoAnn knew from previous conversations how to prepare her conversations with Percy.
6. JoAnn used the ECP approach—expectations, commitments, and permissions

Note: Not in the transcript above, but at the end of the conversation, JoAnn did thank Percy for the time and effort that he had put into finding a solution. It is a good practice, regardless of the outcomes of feedback conversations, to express appreciation when closing the conversation.

Over time, Percy moved to a mentor/coach position with the younger salespeople. He did give up some accounts to do this, but it was a role he discovered that he enjoyed. He gained respect from others, and his help was appreciated and confirmed as sales growth accelerated. And, oh yes, he coaches people on the importance of timely and accurate sales call reports!

5.10   EXPECTATIONS, COMMITMENTS, PERMISSIONS

When feedback is centered on the right side of the feedback criticality continuum that is shown in Figure 5.1, there is an expectation of changed behavior. That change can be directed at the receiver of the feedback. In other situations the receiver may expect some change on the part of the provider in order to support the desired behaviors.

In these conversations, where feedback is intended to be more impactful, it is important that the participants in the feedback conversation are clear about:

1. **Expectations**—Parties to the feedback are clear about expectations:
   - Specific examples of what is expected are provided along with the benefits that can be achieved.
   - Participants paraphrase what the feedback means to them to assure the message was received and understood.
   - It is clear to the parties involved that they know how progress will be measured.
2. **Commitment**—Commitments to agreed expectations are achieved or commitments are modified until agreement is reached:

- Simply telling someone of an expectation does not assure that there is a commitment to meet the expectation. For example, posting team ground rules does not assure that people agreed to or are committed to the ground rules. Confirm that there is a commitment.
- Be specific about what the commitment entails:
  - Time frame
  - Support required
  - Commitments of all parties to the conversation
  - Changes that are a result of the commitment

3. **Permissions**—Consequences of missed commitments are clear:
   - Define the permission given to parties involved when commitments are achieved or not achieved:
     - What are the positive consequences of meeting commitments; benefits to the individual, the team, the organization?
     - What are the consequences of not meeting the commitments? This depends on the circumstances. Often, the permission may be to bring the missed commitments to the attention of the party involved. In other circumstances, particularly in a performance evaluation, the consequences can be more impactful, and these consequences should be clear.

5.11 FEEDBACK IN THE VIRTUAL ENVIRONMENT

Feedback involves a *conversation* between the *provider* and *receiver*, especially when the feedback involves an *expectation of change* and is a *high priority*. Perhaps a brief expression of appreciation bypasses the need for a conversation, but appreciation may morph into a conversation.

Meaningful feedback conversations involve not only words but, more important, body language, eye contact, tone of voice, and gestures that convey perceptions of reality, along with the emotions that those perceptions elicit. Consequential feedback is most effective when it occurs in a face-to-face dialogue, including videoconferencing. It is incumbent on organizations where employees may work remotely that necessary hardware, software, bandwidth, and training are provided to support work in the virtual environment.

5.12   FOCUS AREA UPDATE FOR GIVING FEEDBACK

Do you have additional insights about providing feedback based on the material in Section 5.7 (*Practical Guide for Providing Feedback*), 5.8 (*Three Modes of Feedback*), 5.9 (*Challenging Performance Evaluations*), 5.10 (*Expectations, Commitments, Permissions*), or 5.11 (*Feedback in the Virtual Environment*)? If so, take the opportunity to update your focus areas about giving feedback that you listed previously in this chapter.

FINAL FOCUS AREAS: GIVING FEEDBACK

Focus area 1—Describe a behavior that would improve how you give feedback: (e.g., when people request feedback from me, ask them their opinion of the subject of the feedback prior to giving feedback. This ensures understanding the type of feedback they are requesting):

_____

_____

_____

Focus area 2—Describe a behavior that would improve how you give feedback:

_____

_____

_____

5.13   PRIORITIZING FEEDBACK FOCUS AREAS

In the exercises throughout this chapter you have developed focus areas that would improve your ability to receive and give feedback. From your preceding lists of focus areas, choose no more than three you believe would provide the greatest benefit to you and list them next:

FINAL FOCUS AREAS FOR CHAPTER 5

Highest-priority focus area 1:

_____

_____

_____

Highest-priority focus area 2:

_____

_____

_____

Highest-priority focus area 3:

_____

_____

_____

Don't forget to update the template you downloaded from www.jrosspub .com/CLT to keep track of your focus areas created in exercises throughout this book.

5.14   KEY TAKEAWAYS

1. Feedback about ourselves is essential if we are committed to learning and growing.
2. We can learn from feedback, whether it seems false, unfair, invalid, or poorly delivered. In almost all circumstances, it is important to let people know you appreciate and will consider their feedback. Whether you will take action is another matter for you to decide.
3. Coach the person giving feedback to be *specific*, identify *behaviors* with examples, and explore how the feedback will *impact* you

in relevant and meaningful ways. Learning from feedback about ourselves may require us to develop new behaviors, such as:

- To move from rejection to exploration
- To move from judgment to understanding
- To move from telling to asking
- To move from defending to growing

4. Select focus areas for receiving feedback

5. When giving feedback, apply the SMART technique, engage in conversations to ensure understanding and commitment, and ask people to self-assess to ensure alignment on the purpose of the feedback.

6. When the feedback is requested, consider the scope of consequences (big impact or low impact) in developing the feedback and asking for commitments.

7. When providing unsolicited feedback, request permission before providing it if the expectations contained in the feedback are impactful and include changes in behavior.

8. Prepare for formal feedback, such as performance evaluations, by providing informal feedback often, as appropriate, to avoid surprises. Limit the amount of improvement feedback to the critical few.

9. Consider the ECP technique in situations where specific outcomes are expected.

10. Select focus areas for giving feedback.

11. Prioritize and select focus areas that will have the greatest positive impact on how you receive and give feedback.

ENDNOTES

1. Poertner, Sheila and Karen Massetti Miller. 1996. *The Art of Giving and Receiving Feedback.* New York, NY. American Media Publishing.

2. Stone, Douglas and Shelia Heen. 2017. *Thanks for the Feedback: The Science and Art of Giving and Receiving Feedback.* New York. Penguin Books.

3. Ibid., p. 16.

4. Ibid.

5. Ibid.

6. Ibid., pp. 31–32.
7. Ibid., pp. 28–31.
8. Ibid., pp. 210–211.
9. Holland, Elaine T. 2014. *Making Feedback Work—The Key to Building Effective Teams*. Kindle Edition. pp. 47–48.

CHAPTER 6

EVERY RELATIONSHIP HAS VALUE

"Relationships are based on four principals: respect, under-standing, acceptance, and appreciation."

—Mahatma Gandhi

CHAPTER ROADMAP

The purpose of this chapter is to provide tools and techniques to help you build and strengthen behaviors that will enable *successful relationships*. Why is it important to build successful relationships? The answer may well be obvious, but let us align on why the topic is being brought up here—in a book on communication and leadership. According to Peter Drucker, the purpose of an organization is to satisfy a need we cannot satisfy by ourselves. And, by organization, we mean organization in the broadest sense, including family, the organization where we work, sports teams, communities, etc.—wherever we engage with others to satisfy a need. In most instances, these interactions with other people occur in the context of a relationship. The more successful we are in the relationships we have, the more we are able to satisfy our needs with less time, energy, and stress.

To build upon this fundamental concept of relationships, we will follow a number of steps in the journey through this chapter:

1. Understanding the language of and types of relationships
2. Assessing your relationships
3. Identifying focus areas for improving relationships
4. Creating a relationship-building strategy
5. Identifying enabling behaviors
6. Identifying undermining behaviors
7. Understanding relationship building in the virtual environment
8. Key takeaways of this chapter

6.1   INTRODUCTION—THE LANGUAGE OF RELATIONSHIPS

Relationships can be between and with people, concepts, objects, businesses, etc. In this chapter the focus will be on relationships between and among people. The definition offered by the Free Dictionary by Farlex will serve our purposes:

> *A particular type of connection existing between people related to or having dealings with each other.*[1]

Connections and *dealings* are the operational words in this definition. Connections support relationships and can include mutual interest, necessity, family, and work. Dealings in the context of relationships have to do with how we trade with others to satisfy needs. It may seem off-putting to use the word *trade* in understanding relationships, but we do give in our relationships and expect something tangible or intangible in return. Think about your relationships in the context of Maslow's hierarchy of needs[2] shown in Figure 6.1.

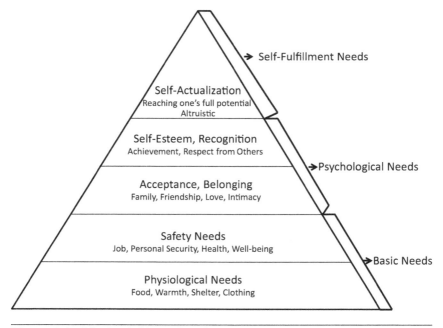

Figure 6.1   Maslow's hierarchy of needs

Let's examine the five levels of needs from Figure 6.1 along with some examples of relationships that may satisfy those needs:

1. **Physiological**—People obtain an income to satisfy basic requirements, including food, shelter, and clothing. We all have connections and dealings with those who help satisfy basic needs. These needs may be satisfied by others with whom we trade for goods and essential services.

2. **Safety**—Work can satisfy needs for order, predictability, and control (i.e., safety and security). These safety and personal security needs can be satisfied by police, safety equipment, and medical professionals.

3. **Belonging**—These needs may be satisfied by connections at work, in our community, and with friends. Intimate personal relationships may satisfy our need for love.

4. **Esteem**—The need for recognition and the feeling of accomplishment may be satisfied at work and working in one's community, church, and neighborhood.

5. **Self-actualization**—The need to reach a person's full potential may be satisfied by relationships with mentors, coaches, and teachers. Altruistic needs may be met by working for charitable organizations in countries with unmet needs (e.g., Doctors Without Borders).

There are two key points to be made from this analysis. The first point is that, with few exceptions, the needs that were promulgated by Maslow are fulfilled through connections and dealings with others (i.e., relationships). We can represent the connection between needs fulfillment and relationships by the formula:

Needs fulfillment = F (relationships)

The second point pertains to building on the importance of relationships to satisfying needs; imagine a continuum of types of relationships using the variable of *needs satisfied*. At one end of the continuum, there are few, if any, connections or dealings with others, and there is a low level of needs satisfied (e.g., no relationships exist). At the other end of the continuum, there are a myriad of connections and dealings where important needs are satisfied (e.g., deep relationships). This continuum of relationships is show in Figure 6.2, where one axis is the need to be satisfied and the other axis represents the time required to build and maintain those relationships.

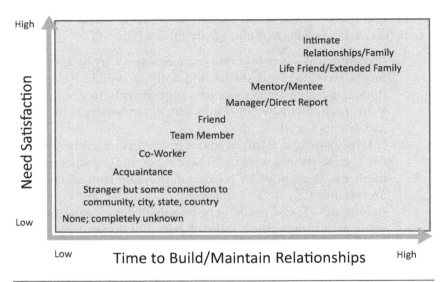

Figure 6.2　The relationship time-commitment continuum

The message of Figure 6.2 is that building relationships takes time, and time is the most important resource we have. It is irreplaceable. Time for proactively building relationships is a scarce resource today, considering the tsunami of opportunities for relationships brought about by the social media applications on our smartphones, in addition to demands on our time from family, friends, community, work, hobbies, etc.

Often, the important tasks in our lives are overwhelmed by the urgent. Consequently, the building of relationships requires *habits* that "automatically" put us into relationship-building mode without having to think about it.

A key takeaway of this chapter is for you to identify key relationships and the needs satisfied in those target relationships. Before we do that, we need to review your own experience with relationships in order to provide input for how you will build relationships going forward.

6.2　AN ASSESSMENT OF YOUR RELATIONSHIPS

In this section you are going to describe both impactful, fulfilling relationships and those that lacked these characteristics. Consider these characteristics of good relationships as you describe your experiences:

1. **Trust**—People in the relationship trust each other to be truthful, fulfill their commitments, not gossip about each other, etc.
2. **Mutual respect**—People involved in the relationship respect the opinions of others, along with their religious beliefs, race, and culture.
3. **Give and take**—Parties to the relationship receive benefits and give back to the relationship.
4. **Transparency**—There is open communication in the relationship and no hidden agendas.
5. **Appreciation**—Parties in the relationship acknowledge the contribution of people who give toward building the relationship.

Now, list no more than two relationships that have been or are now productive, satisfying, and impactful in some sense. Describe why this relationship is positive. List the characteristics of those relationships (e.g., open and honest, you can say anything, not judgmental, able to disagree, etc.). Describe specifically what you are doing or what you did to enable, enhance, or contribute to that relationship being impactful. Consider the needs that these relationships satisfy.

Relationship 1—Describe the relationship (e.g., family member, colleague at work) and the characteristics, including the needs satisfied, that make it a meaningful relationship for you:

_____

_____

_____

What do you do to contribute to the positive nature of this relationship?

_____

_____

_____

Relationship 2—Describe the relationship (e.g., family member, colleague at work) and the characteristics, including the needs satisfied, that make it a meaningful relationship for you:

_____

_____

_____

What do you do to contribute to the positive nature of this relationship?

_____

_____

_____

Now, list no more than two relationships that have not been or at this time are not satisfying, or are stressful, unproductive, or negative. Describe why this relationship was not, or is not, satisfying. List the characteristics of these relationships (e.g., the other person is judgmental, selfish, or close-minded). Describe specifically what you have done, or are doing, to contribute to the status of this relationship. That is to say, what behaviors do you own?

Relationship 1—Describe the relationship (e.g., family member, colleague at work) and the characteristics, including unmet needs, that make it dissatisfying/not impactful:

_____

_____

_____

What have you done, or are doing now, that is contributing to the status of this relationship?

_____

_____

_____

Relationship 2—Describe the relationship (e.g., family member, colleague at work) and the characteristics, including unmet needs, that make it dissatisfying/not impactful:

_____

_____

_____

What have you done, or are doing now, that is contributing to the status of this relationship?

_____

_____

_____

From the foregoing analyses, do certain behaviors stand out? Behaviors you should do more of, less of, start doing, or stop doing? If so, take the opportunity to list no more than two focus areas in which you want to change a behavior in order to improve your relationships with others.

FOCUS AREAS FOR CHAPTER 6

Focus area 1—Describe a behavior that would improve your relationships with others (e.g., demonstrate respect for the opinions of others when working to solve problems):

_____

_____

_____

Focus area 2—Describe a behavior that would improve your relationships with others:

_____

_____

_____

Don't forget to update the template you downloaded from www.jrosspub .com/CLT to keep track of your focus areas created in exercises throughout this book.

6.3   GOING FORWARD: CREATE A RELATIONSHIP-BUILDING STRATEGY

6.3.1   Who—Identify Key Relationships

Develop a list of people (no more than three) with whom you desire to build or strengthen a relationship. Avoid choosing people who agree with you, exhibit biases, or provide friendly rather than accurate feedback. Instead, choose people who will challenge you so that both of you will get something from the relationship. Here is a starter list:

1. People at work
2. Friends
3. Professional associates
4. Mentors/coaches

5. Family/extended family
6. Romantic interests
7. Customers/vendors
8. Elected/appointed officials
9. Neighbors/community/church members

Under each name, list no more than two needs that you expect this relationship to satisfy (what's in it for you) and what needs the other party can expect to satisfy in the relationship (what's in it for them). As you go through your list, you may find yourself replacing names or otherwise adjusting your list as you think through the purpose of the relationship from everyone's perspective.

EXAMPLE:
Relationship 1: Coworker

Needs I have—*Complete their work as expected, give me feedback on how I can help them complete their work, contribute to a friendly environment, and show appreciation when I help them.*

Needs they have—*I complete my work product, provide feedback to the department manager when my coworker does something well, and provide feedback to my coworker if they are not meeting expectations.*

YOUR LIST:

Relationship 1: _____

    Needs I have: _____

    _____

    _____

    Needs they have: _____

    _____

    _____

Relationship 2: _____

    Needs I have: _____

    _____

    _____

    Needs they have: _____

    _____

    _____

Relationship 3: _____

    Needs I have: _____

    _____

    _____

    Needs they have: _____

    _____

    _____

At this point, do not be concerned that your list is somewhat incomplete or imperfect. The purpose is to think about your needs and the needs of the people in your relationships.

6.3.2 How—Plan How You Will Build Relationships

The objective of this section is to construct a plan to assist with building relationships with the people whom you have identified. Remember that relationships are about connections and it is best to build relationships *before* you need them. Ways to connect may include any of the following:

1. Mutual interests
   - Athletic activities such as biking, tennis, golf, hiking, or walking
   - Family activities/connections such as children's schools, alumni associations, neighborhood events, or events at church
   - Artistic/social events including concerts, art shows, museums, plays, or ballet
   - Hobbies including cars, stamps, chess, mahjong, or card games
   - Activities involving food and beverages
   - Current events such as politics, climate change, immigration, etc.
2. Work-related activities
   - Project work
   - Professional organizations
   - Lunches, coffee, or after-work events in the community
   - Activities under mutual interests

List ways you will build connections with each person on your relationship list. Describe what you will do to build the relationship and estimate the time that you will give toward building the relationship. Modify or adjust the number of relationships on your list until the time that your plan requires coincides with the time that is available. Keep in mind however, if you don't have (or take) time now, you may be spending more time later working through issues with people where a relationship is poor or nonexistent.

EXAMPLE:

Relationship 1: A manager in another department who controls resources

Connections—Children go to the same school.

Relationship-building activities—Connect at school functions, participate in parent activities at school, discuss children's activities and experiences during informal coffee breaks; these efforts may lead to other connections.

Time needed (estimate hours per week, month, or other measure of time)—*Two to three hours per month.*

YOUR LIST:

Relationship 1: _____

    Connections: _____

    Relationship-building activities: _____

    _____

    _____

    Time needed (estimate hours per week, month, or other measure of

    time): _____

    _____

Relationship 2: _____

    Connections: _____

    Relationship-building activities: _____

    _____

    _____

    Time needed (estimate hours per week, month, or other measure of

    time): _____

    _____

Relationship 3: _____

    Connections: _____

Relationship-building activities: _____

_____

_____

Time needed (estimate hours per week, month, or other measure of

time): _____

_____

There is a template provided in Appendix B if you prefer a more robust plan than the notional lists presented here. You can also use the calendar in your email application or smartphone to schedule activities.

TIME COMMITMENTS

We have been working on specific relationship-building strategies so you can practice behaviors that will eventually become habits. However, you may have other activities in your personal and work life that will require your focus. Be reasonable with your efforts, time, and energy when attempting to build these specific relationships. Do not overextend and take on too many.

6.4   RELATIONSHIP ENABLERS

The purpose of the connecting activities you have listed in your relationship-building plan is to provide an opportunity to have conversations that will build and strengthen your relationships. These conversations can be about aspects of your activities, such as golf scores; project work; family activities; and/or reactions to theater performances, concerts, etc. The following list suggests other types of conversations and behaviors that may help you build connections:

1. Bring suggested solutions to problems to meetings
2. Be open and share information about yourself when the time is right (tell people about yourself and ask about them)
3. Keep your commitments

4. Share credit for accomplishments or ideas
5. Avoid gossiping
6. Practice active listening
7. Remember things that are important to others
8. Be consistent and manage emotions
9. Invite people to become involved; ask for their opinion
10. Extend yourself and go out of your way to help others (at least once in a while)

6.5 RELATIONSHIP INHIBITORS

Relationship inhibitors are the opposite of the enablers in the previous list. Inhibitors include:

1. **Too many relationships**—As was stated in the introduction of this chapter, we are overwhelmed with opportunities for relationships caused by social media, emails, text messages, etc. In fact, to manage our time commitments, we have become more proficient at turning away from relationship-building opportunities (e.g., not listening, not engaging, or engaging superficially). Robin Dunbar is known for the *Dunbar Number*.[3] He theorized that the number of people that individuals can realistically manage and engage in a social network is 150. Whether or not that number is exact, Dunbar causes us to consider the number of relationships that we are supporting. When we talk about meaningful relationships where mutual needs are satisfied (going back to Figure 6.2), the number of *significant* relationships may be far less than Dunbar's 150. If you do not have the time to devote to relationships, those relationships will most likely suffer.

2. **Relationship decay**—Consequently, the question as to how many relationships can be supported is hindered by the fact that relationships tend to decay over time without continual nurturing. It is preferred that the decay is intentional rather than a matter of forgetfulness or time management. One solution is to maintain a library or *database* of relationships going from casual all the way up to intimate. Some people will use their smartphones to *ping* them a reminder to spend the time needed on building high-priority relationships, especially in the early stages. While this may seem like overkill, the exercise will help build the desired

habits. Of course, a phone call, holiday card, or text message can also be an appropriate way to maintain important relationships.

3. **The *I* word is the *termite* of relationships**—Relationships that are centered on one person will not survive for long. When people demonstrate a lack of interest in others, they are signaling that the others are not important, and neither is the relationship.

4. **Lack of respect**—Lack of respect for the other participants in a relationship (e.g., their opinion, their beliefs, their culture, etc.) undermines relationships. You do not have to agree, but it is imperative to show respect in your relationships.

6.6   BUILDING/MAINTAINING RELATIONSHIPS IN THE VIRTUAL ENVIRONMENT

The importance of relationships is independent of whether people are working in a physical or virtual environment. Likewise, the communication process presented in Figure 2.1 is relevant in either environment. There are, however, considerations when building and maintaining relationships in the virtual environment.

1. The tools of the virtual environment, including text, Facebook, Twitter, blogs, email, etc., provide opportunities to *connect* with a vast audience. As was pointed out earlier in this chapter, relationships take time to build and maintain. Figure 6.2 makes the point that the time required for a relationship increases as the needs met by the relationship increases, and needs are not a function of whether people are in the physical or virtual environment. One can convincingly argue that the tools of the virtual environment allow needs to be satisfied more efficiently with less time. This may be true up to a point. However, we encourage you to be alert to the time commitment that is necessary to nurture relationships and to manage the number of your relationships. You should allow for time to participate in relationships that are a priority in the sense that they satisfy a variety of important needs.

2. The tools available to facilitate communication in the virtual environment are efficient yet may lack the effectiveness of face-to-face communications. Experts say that 80% of communication occurs nonverbally, including through tone of voice, eye contact,

and body language.[4] The following list explains some best practices for building and maintaining relationships in the virtual environment:[5]

- Provide guidelines and training to help people learn how to use available tools to have productive conversations with people they know and to build relationships with peers and experts throughout the organization.
- Look for opportunities to discuss topics outside of the work environment. Share personal information, including educational experience, hobbies, travel, and successes of family members. Encourage others to share stories about themselves and family members.
- Make time for face time. Use video conferencing whenever possible when people are not colocated. The organization can provide video conferencing tools and training for employees who are working in a virtual environment.
- Look for opportunities to meet face-to-face. While in-person meetings may be difficult with a global team, search for opportunities where some, if not all, of the team members can meet.
- Look for opportunities for *fun* activities in the virtual environment, including non-work-related virtual groups, chats, and events that can help employees experiment with collaboration tools while connecting with colleagues beyond their own teams and home offices.
- Create a *safe environment* where people can express concerns, challenges, and disagreements with others by:
  - Demonstrating trustworthiness through active listening, avoiding judgmental comments, creating team ground rules that define appropriate behaviors both inside and outside of meetings, and granting permission to bring up sensitive issues to team members.
  - Respecting the opinions of others. Whether or not people agree with those opinions is another matter.
  - Focusing on what is said and not on who said it.

Safety in the virtual environment is important because research shows that virtual teammates are two-and-a-half times more likely to perceive mistrust, incompetence, broken commitments, and bad decision making with distant colleagues than those who are colocated. Worse, they report taking five to 10 times longer to address their concerns.[6]

6.7   KEY TAKEAWAYS

Key takeaways from this chapter include:

1. We have relationships to satisfy our needs.
2. There is a continuum of relationships, extending from perfunctory, casual, work, and social, to intimate. These relationships require more time, energy, and commitment as we move up the continuum shown in Figure 6.1.
3. Many of us have built relationships without much conscious thought and perhaps not much energy (e.g., friendships we have had from early school years). As we have grown and the opportunity for relationships appears limitless, a more conscious effort (a strategy, so to speak) is needed to strengthen/build important and impactful relationships.
4. The development of habits to build and maintain relationships will require you to exercise the specific behaviors needed to build those habits.
5. You have developed a plan to build and strengthen relationships with no more than three people whom you identified in Section 6.3.1. When you plan to change your behaviors in a relationship, it may be a good idea to inform the relationship *partner* about the change and the purpose of the change.

ENDNOTES

1. *Relationships*. Retrieved February 5, 2021, from the Free Dictionary by Farlex at https://www.thefreedictionary.com/relationship.
2. Maslow, Andrew. 1943. "A Theory of Human Motivation." *Psychological Review* 50, no. 4. pp. 370–396.
3. Dunbar, Robin. 1992. "Neocortex Size as a Constraint on Group Size in Primates." *Journal of Human Evolution* 22, no. 6. pp. 469–493.

4. Thompson, Jeff. 2011. "Is Nonverbal Communication a Numbers Game? Is Body Language Really over 90% of How We Communicate?" Retrieved June 3, 2021, from *Psychology Today* at https://www.psychologytoday.com/us/blog/beyond-words/201109/is-nonverbal-communication-numbers-game.

5. "Building Relationships in the Virtual Workplace." 2021. Retrieved May 16, 2021, from the *American Productivity and Quality Center* at https://www.apqc.org/system/files/resource-file/2021-01/K011208%20Building%20Relationships%20in%20the%20Virtual%20Workplace.pdf.

6. Grenny, Joseph. 2017. "How to Raise Sensitive Issues During a Virtual Meeting." Retrieved May 20, 2021, from *Harvard Business Review* at https://hbr.org/2017/03/how-to-raise-sensitive-issues-during-a-virtual-meeting.

CHAPTER 7

CONSEQUENTIAL COMMUNICATION

"Let us make a special effort to stop communicating with each other, so we can have some conversation."

—Mark Twain

CHAPTER ROADMAP

This chapter aims to examine the process of having meaningful discussions, which often occur during a meeting with another person or a small group of people. We refer to these talks as *necessary* because the resulting consequences, whether favorable or harmful, are substantial for the individuals who are participating or are influenced by the conversation's outcome. The majority of us have experienced relationships that were irrevocably altered by a single chat. A single discussion has the potential to shape your career, your organization's future, the course of a project, and the lives of many stakeholders (employees, investors, management, suppliers, and more). A single conversation can impact your life and the personal lives of others. In addition, you may be unaware that a specific interaction is crucial and has significant ramifications. A casual chat might evolve into a vital one. It would help if you kept in mind that every conversation might become a critical one. This is especially true when more senior members of the organization are involved or when speaking with peers. The following information is a roadmap for the critical conversation process that we will follow in this chapter, which emphasizes discussions with more senior executives (communicating up the organization) or peer group members (communicating across the organization):

1. Perform an assessment
2. Plan the conversation

3. Conduct the conversation
4. Close the conversation
5. Focus area updates

7.1 PERFORM AN ASSESSMENT

Before the meeting in which the discussion will take place, analyze the meeting's context, including the *situation*, the *relationship*, the *message*, the *sender*, and the *receiver*, along with the *channel* and *expected results* from the perspective of each participant. Even if the dialogue is spontaneous, make a mental note of those components. Analyze each component and identify potential possibilities and dangers before the discussion. The following are lists of questions that were designed to prepare you for the forthcoming meeting:

1. **The situation**
   - What is the purpose of the meeting from each participant's viewpoint?
   - What is the importance of the conversation (e.g., why are we meeting) from each participant's perspective (refer back to Figure 5.1)?
   - If the conversation goes well, list desired outcomes from each person attending the meeting:

     ▫ Yourself: _____

     ▫ Participant 1: _____

     ▫ Participant 2: _____

   - If the conversation does not go well, list the consequences from the participants' perspectives:

     ▫ Yourself: _____

     ▫ Participant 1: _____

     ▫ Participant 2: _____

- Has something happened recently that might affect the participants in the meeting (e.g., a project taking a turn for the worse, regulatory changes that impact the organization, changing market conditions, etc.)?
- Why are you being asked to participate?
  - ◻ If the meeting is about the performance of your team, an individual on your team, or your own performance, be prepared to explain the circumstances and the activities that you are taking to enhance performance.
  - ◻ Do you intend to submit a request for a team member's promotion, compensation modification, or extra resources? When addressing a request to a senior executive, the easiest and most straightforward response you are likely to get is, "No." A "yes" answer will place them in the position of justifying their decision to others who may then make similar requests or argue against the decision. As a result, when requesting anything from a senior executive, outline the implications of their refusal to say "yes." Then make it simple for them to say "yes" by giving them the necessary knowledge to handle those consequences.

In assessing the situation, you should also consider potential barriers to having an effective conversation. Some barriers to consider include the following:

- **Barriers to listening** (see Chapter 4):
  - ◻ *Culture*: Are there any cultural differences you should consider when conducting this conversation, such as age, gender, religion, or class position? If so, be attentive to those areas during the discussion (e.g., through body language, eye contact, etc.).
  - ◻ *Knowledge base*: Is there a shared understanding of the knowledge required for the conversation? If one of the participants has a superior domain expertise to the other, the dialogue may get disconnected. This is especially true when speaking with senior executives, who often have a larger view of the business and its plethora of moving pieces and interdependencies, and with the market and competitors. Due to their larger

perspective, what is considered a priority for you may not be a priority for them.

- *Emotional state*: If you encounter someone who is distracted by circumstances, impatient, or dynamic, it may be prudent to reschedule or postpone the talk, especially with a peer or more senior individual.
- *Personality*: Individual personalities may pose impediments that should be taken into account. Recall the discussion in Chapter 3 of personality types and their effect on communication (e.g., Outgoing versus Reserved personalities).

2. **The relationship**—Analyze the relationship between the participants in the dialogue. Is this a more official or casual relationship? What is at risk in the relationship, whether the discussion is successful or unsuccessful? Consider any purpose you may have for advancing or enhancing the connection as part of your assessment. Chapter 6 is devoted to relationship building with the premise that partnerships exist to meet needs. When scheduling a meeting with another party, list the demands that the other party expects you to meet and then determine what demands you need to meet for the other party.

3. **The message**—Assess the contents of your message. The message should be clear in your mind because this will guide you to ensure that you have a fruitful conversation.

4. **The sender**—Evaluate the sender (i.e., the initiator of the conversation). If you respond to a meeting request and are unfamiliar with the initiator, get as much information as possible in order to do an initial evaluation. For instance, you may like to learn about the individual's background, demeanor, amount of influence, and any other information that can aid you in organizing the dialogue. In certain instances, the talk may serve as a springboard for initiating a relationship (consider the importance, which we covered in Chapter 6). Always ask yourself, "What's in it for the initiator?" and "Why is this conversation or meeting being initiated?"

5. **The receiver**—If you initiated the communication, examine all of the points that you outlined previously for the sender. In addition, consider the receiver's opinion of you and the purpose of the conversation.

6. **The channel**—Consider the venue for your talk or gathering. If it is to be a face-to-face meeting, dress appropriately. If the chat takes place virtually, prepare any necessary papers and familiarize yourself with the instrument that will be utilized (Zoom, GoTo Meeting, Google Meet, etc.). It is a certainty that virtual gatherings will be utilized more and more in the future. Ascertain that your devices and software are functioning correctly and that you have the necessary internet speed to collaborate remotely. Knowing the specifics enables you to organize the conversation or encounter more effectively.

7. **The result (outcome)**—If you start the conversation or meeting, be particular about the desired outcome or result; this will assist you while preparing the talk or session and also during the actual discussion or meeting. If you are responding to a meeting request, make every effort to comprehend the *why* of the conversation.

7.2   PLAN THE CONVERSATION

After evaluating the situation, plan the discussion in order to handle it more efficiently (instead of being managed). Lead the way by having a strategy in place, but avoid impeding the discourse by dictating or micromanaging it. The following recommendations can assist you in organizing your conversation:

1. Create an outline for your opening statements or *icebreakers*. If you're conversing with someone whom you don't know well, come up with some starting remarks or questions to kick-start a friendly and healthy conversation.

2. Ensure that all participants in the conversation agree on the conversation's aim and desired conclusion. Depending on the authority and/or cultural norms of the individuals involved in the talk, it may be prudent to postpone starting the topic and seek clarity rather than announcing the meeting's objective. Suppose you think that the time provided for the talk is insufficient to accomplish all the desired goals. In that case, you can recommend a subset to focus on during the meeting and offer follow-up sessions to agree on other objectives. Define or assist in defining the desired results, particularly from other participants' perspectives,

and decide on the repercussions for those attending if the desired goals are not realized.

3. Is it possible to plan the details of the conversation? When, where, and how? Are there any minor elements that require attention? Often, it is the seemingly minor details that have the most influence. These essential dialogues typically take place during meetings. Agree on the time, date, location, and agenda for such meetings.

4. With the evaluation in mind, prepare your questions in advance. As you consider which questions to ask, take on the role of the devil's advocate.

5. Take into account any possible *trigger* words (words that may spark a reaction). Trigger words can include any word or phrase frequently used, such as change, disruption, hatred, love, control, out of control, wish, and any other term or phrase. Prepare your response to these words in advance. Consider utilizing the echo approach explained in Chapter 4.

6. Consider the responses to possible inquiries. List the tough questions (the ones you hope will not be asked) and be prepared to answer them or perhaps even offer them before they are asked.

7. Contemplate conducting a dry run or rehearsal with a coworker.

Finally, and perhaps most important, if the conversation has the potential to become emotionally charged or toxic, be prepared to address how the person feels, keep the relationship in focus rather than the outcome, focus on solutions rather than problems, be firm, and establish boundaries regarding what can and cannot be decided. At the most extreme, call a halt to the meeting and/or take a break to allow participants to regroup and refocus.

Preparing for a conversation in advance offers you an advantage. The better prepared you are, the more successfully you can steer the conversation toward a positive conclusion.

7.3 CONDUCT THE CONVERSATION

Consider all of the listening and questioning strategies mentioned before while you lead or engage in the conversation. Others may begin the dialogue, depending on their organizational roles, power, and cultural norms. If the conditions allow you to take the initiative, start with your icebreakers or beginning comments. Communicate your message or messages without assuming control of the conversation. Be considerate to the other participants in the discourse. Utilize your listening abilities to detect *key* or *trigger* words. Adopt any strategy that you discovered during preparation to address those key terms. Do not be afraid to ask *why*, particularly if you hear a repeated word or phrase. Utilize open-ended inquiries to peel back the onion of a topic or position and go further into it.

Consider both your aim and the objectives of the other parties. If a discussion veers off track, you may need to redirect it back to the topic's original intent. A frequently used strategy for efficiently organizing meetings is establishing a *parking lot* for off-agenda items. In a discussion, you might use a similar approach by accepting the point stated but then asking if the subject may be discussed later.

7.4   CLOSE THE CONVERSATION

When concluding the conversation, make an effort to do it *cleanly* without leaving any loose ends. Summarize or paraphrase the dialogue or its conclusion. Inquire about the summary's accuracy. If choices have been taken, ensure that they are agreed upon. In those situations where you may not agree on a choice or decision, try to obtain confirmation that you "agree to disagree" or perhaps postpone the decision to a future discussion. Be concise and detailed in your description of any action items or future steps. If a written follow-up is necessary, establish who will do it and how. If you plan to give follow-up, do it as soon as feasible (a general guideline is to provide written follow-up within 24 hours).

Always attempt to end on a positive note. While the outcome may not always be as planned, it is critical to end on a high note for the relationship's sake.

In addition, you might consider conducting your assessment of the interaction. What was successful? Was your preconversation analysis and planning fruitful? What could you have done more effectively? What would you do differently if you could redo the discussion (or even a follow-up conversation)? In addition, if feasible, solicit opinions from other parties involved.

7.5 CASE EXERCISE

You are Richard's mentor. Richard was just appointed to the position of manager of an engineering team and is inexperienced with leadership. You run a separate department but agreed to mentor Richard informally because he is a buddy and desires to join the leadership team. Linda, vice president of the marketing department, has sought a meeting with Richard to get to know him better. The marketing department relies on communication updates from the engineering department in order to organize marketing campaigns efficiently. Richard is aware that the marketing department frequently complains about the engineering team's inability to communicate effectively.

Using the information in this chapter, describe how you may assist Richard in preparing for his meeting with Linda.

_____

_____

_____

_____

_____

7.6 FOCUS AREA UPDATE FOR CONSEQUENTIAL COMMUNICATION

Review the lessons in this chapter and consider the following:

1. Take into account any impactful interactions. Choose at least one exchange that might occur in an *informal* context (such as a dinner or networking event) and at least one conversation that may happen in a *formal* setting. Consider how you would prepare for an informal chat. Document what went well and what might have been done better following the conversation. In addition, consider what you may do differently in a future comparable circumstance. Then, employ the method to facilitate a more formal discussion and document the conclusion. Your growth must

ascertain why you were or were not successful in obtaining your desired goals. Your analysis may reveal areas where you need further experience with the process in order to continue developing your communication abilities. If you successfully attained your objectives, assess what worked and determine how to replicate your achievement.

2. Based on the insights acquired from the information in this chapter, list your focus areas for improving consequential communication.

FOCUS AREAS FOR CHAPTER 7

Focus area 1—Describe a behavior that would improve consequential communication (e.g., in planning for a conversation with my supervisor about progress on deliverables, gather metrics to define progress and areas for improvement):

_____

_____

_____

Focus area 2—Describe a behavior that would improve consequential communication:

_____

_____

_____

Don't forget to update the template you downloaded from www.jross pub.com/CLT to keep track of your focus areas created in exercises throughout this book.

7.7   KEY TAKEAWAYS

The key takeaways from this chapter include the following:

1. A conversation is a four-step process: assessment, planning, conducting, and closing.

2. A proper assessment can significantly impact the quality and results of the conversation.
3. Plan as much as you can to ensure an effective conversation.
4. Manage and control the conversation to ensure the objectives are met. Use your listening and questioning skills to manage the conversation.
5. Close the conversation cleanly and end on a positive note.

CHAPTER 8

MINING DISAGREEMENTS FOR VALUE

"In the middle of difficulty lies opportunity."

—Albert Einstein

CHAPTER ROADMAP

We appear to be drowning in a sea of disagreements about the political, health, and social spheres of our lives (e.g., southern border crisis, response to COVID-19, and income disparity, to name but a few). We add to this list the more common, but just as impactful to us as individuals, disagreements at work (resource allocation) and in our personal lives (among family members, friends, neighbors, etc.). Einstein's wisdom reminds us that difficulty (aka disagreements) can result in capturing opportunities. There are avenues that can lead to better outcomes rather than simply being stuck defending the same old positions. Sometimes people are open to moving forward with a new plan rather than defending the old one.

The purpose of this chapter is first to recognize the value that can come from disagreements and then to provide tools and techniques that will help you *mine* those disagreements for value. The roadmap we will follow in this chapter to achieve these goals is outlined here:

1. Define disagreements/conflicts
2. Assess your experiences with disagreements/conflict
3. Describe focus areas based on experiences with disagreements/conflicts
4. When to resolve disagreements (before they become full-blown conflicts)
5. Your role in resolving disagreements
6. Strategies for resolving disagreements/conflicts

7. Checklist for responses to disagreements
8. Update focus areas for obtaining value from disagreeing well
9. Key takeaways

8.1 INTRODUCTION: WHAT ARE DISAGREEMENTS/CONFLICTS?

You will encounter the word *disagreements* in this chapter more often than *conflicts* because disagreements occur more frequently than emotionally charged conflicts. In addition, it is important to build a mindset. The word conflict is dramatic; it implies a deadlock, something difficult to resolve, and something that you must win (or cannot lose). The term disagreement is less emotionally charged; it connotes more openness and less risk.

As you become involved in situations where people have different opinions, beliefs, or perceptions, approach them as disagreements rather than conflicts and the conversations that follow will likely change. You will signal openness with a willingness to listen and understand the other parties' position. They, in turn, are more likely to mirror those behaviors to everyone's benefit.

Mining value from disagreements is based upon two premises:

1. The organization and team both benefit from informed, rigorous, unfiltered debate on issues of importance:
   • Exploring disagreements around concepts, ideas, decisions, and differing priorities can lead to better outcomes.
   • Open and straightforward discussion of differences leads to learning and skill development of team members that is necessary for them to grow into leadership roles.
2. Avoiding disagreements undermines the creation of value for the organization:
   • Avoiding disagreements undermines team members' opportunity to learn how to disagree well and manage/leverage disagreements/conflicts, which is a necessary leadership skill.
   • Avoiding disagreements in the name of *saving time* actually causes more time to be spent on addressing the disagreement again and again down the road.
   • Unresolved disagreements can fester and harm relationships when team members believe their views have not had an opportunity to be heard.

- Unresolved disagreements can escalate into emotional outbursts, destructive competition, and hidden agendas, and may cause team members to withdraw from future discussions involving disagreements.
- The organization/team loses an opportunity to learn how to debate, discuss, and grow by redirecting energy from people to issues.

Disagreements can occur whenever people have different values, motivations, perceptions, ideas, or priorities. Sometimes these differences appear trivial, but when disagreements trigger strong feelings, a deep personal *need* is often at the root of the problem. These needs can range from the need to feel safe, secure, respected, and/or valued, to the need for greater closeness and intimacy.

A representation of disagreements is shown on a continuum of disagreements in Figure 8.1. Although much of the literature focuses on the *conflict side* of the continuum, many disagreements are more in the middle to the left side of the continuum. Learning how to disagree well can help keep you on the left side of the continuum where acceptable resolutions are more likely in shorter periods of time and with better outcomes. While this chapter addresses the entire continuum, the emphasis is on how to disagree well.

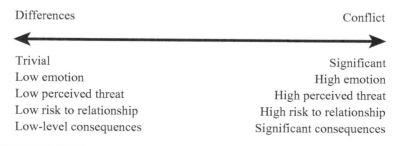

Differences	Conflict
Trivial	Significant
Low emotion	High emotion
Low perceived threat	High perceived threat
Low risk to relationship	High risk to relationship
Low-level consequences	Significant consequences

Figure 8.1   The disagreement continuum

8.2   AN ASSESSMENT OF YOUR EXPERIENCES WITH DISAGREEMENTS

List two situations in the space provided where you have had a disagreement and the outcome was satisfactory, keeping these factors in mind:

1. The resolution was acceptable to the parties involved (perhaps not necessarily optimal for either party).
2. The time and energy required to reach a resolution did not overshadow the benefit.
3. Relationships were strengthened.
4. You gained a customer or some other business benefit.
5. You gained insight and learnings from how the disagreement was managed.
6. You prevented the trivial from morphing into the significant.

Experience 1—Describe the disagreement, whom it involved (family member, client, colleague at work, etc.), and the outcome that was satisfactory/beneficial:

_____

_____

_____

What did you do to contribute to the meaningful outcome?

_____

_____

_____

Experience 2—Describe the disagreement, whom it involved (family member, client, colleague at work, etc.), and the outcome that was satisfactory/beneficial:

_____

_____

What did you do to contribute to the meaningful outcome?

_____

_____

_____

Now think of two situations where you had a disagreement and the outcomes were *not* satisfactory in the sense that:

1. A resolution acceptable to the parties was not achieved.
2. The disagreement resulted in extra work.
3. The disagreement resulted in strained relationships or other negative consequences.
4. You lost a customer or vendor, or had another negative business impact.
5. The trivial escalated to the significant.

Experience 1—Describe the disagreement, whom it involved (family member, client, colleague at work, etc.), and the outcome, or lack of the desired outcome (e.g., the benefit that was not achieved):

_____

_____

_____

What did you do, or not do, that contributed to the experience?

_____

_____

_____

Experience 2—Describe the disagreement, whom it involved (family member, client, colleague at work, etc.), and the outcome, or lack of the desired outcome (e.g., the benefit that was not achieved):

_____

_____

_____

What did you do, or not do, that contributed to the experience?

_____

_____

_____

Do certain behaviors stand out from the experiences you outlined? Are there behaviors you should do more of, less of, start doing, or stop doing? If so, take the opportunity to list no more than two focus areas where you want to change your behavior to improve your ability to disagree well.

INITIAL FOCUS AREAS FOR CHAPTER 8

Focus area 1—Describe a behavior that would improve your ability to disagree well and mine value from disagreements (e.g., recognize that I often feel I have to win when I disagree with someone):

_____

_____

Focus area 2—Describe a behavior that would improve your ability to disagree well and mine value from disagreements:

_____

_____

8.3   WHEN SHOULD YOU RESOLVE DISAGREEMENTS?

The literature about resolving disagreements/conflicts is abundant, including the following titles:

1. Six Steps to Conflict Resolution in the Workplace[1]
2. 10 Tips for Resolving Conflict[2]
3. 11 Ways You Can Better Resolve Conflicts[3]

Most of these methods include a first step to communicate that the problem exists and then to describe what the conflict is about. Throughout the literature on conflict resolution, the recommendation is to resolve the conflict as soon as possible. The underlying premise is that the longer the conflict exists, the more likely the protagonists will freeze on their positions. Thus, it becomes more difficult to resolve the disagreement and/or opportunities for a better solution will expire where only less optimal solutions remain. In addition, relationships may suffer, or the conflict will go *underground* where it festers. When the participants in a trivial disagreement allow it to go unattended, it is more likely the disagreement will escalate into conflict.

The relationship between time to reach resolution and the ability to reach a resolution is presented in the graph shown in Figure 8.2.

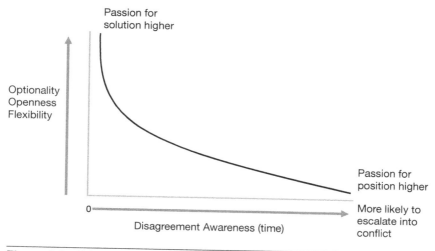

Figure 8.2   When do you manage disagreements? Version 1

The conclusion reached from this graph is that when disagreements occur, address them as soon as possible. And this is true, but we recommend a modification to that conclusion: address/resolve disagreements before they occur! You are probably wondering how people can resolve disagreements when they don't exist. Consider the following:

1. You know that you are going to have disagreements in your personal and work environments.
2. You are more able to resolve differences with people you know, people you trust. That is to say, people with whom you have a relationship.

Given these points, we recommend that you build relationships with people whom you are likely to have disagreements. Examples include the following:

1. *The owners of resources, either human or capital*—they may have other priorities when you need those resources for a project at work.
2. *The mothers of the bride and groom*—who will likely have different preferences for the wedding arrangements.
3. *Members of neighborhood associations*—who are likely to disagree about where to spend limited budgets.
4. *People who prefer to work alone* and *people who prefer to work in groups*—these work style differences can cause differences of opinions when collaboration is needed to solve a problem.

The point being, you are more likely to resolve differences when you have *relationships* with people. Build relationships before you need them. Now the graph changes to appear as shown in Figure 8.3.

When you resolve differences quickly, they are likely to remain as simple disagreements rather than escalating into conflicts. Everyone knows they are going to have disagreements in their personal and work environments. Consequently, build relationships with people with whom you are likely to have disagreements.

Revisit Section 6.3 where you listed people with whom you want to build relationships. Modify that list if there are relationships you will need in the future that you do not have now. Start building those relationships.

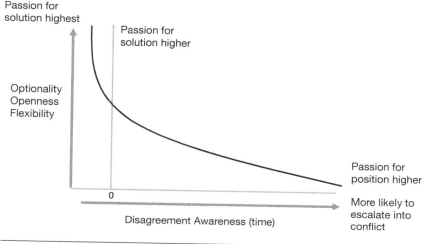

Figure 8.3   When do you manage disagreements? Version 2

8.4   WHAT CAN YOU DO TO MANAGE DISAGREEMENTS/CONFLICTS?

While the behaviors to resolve disagreements and conflicts are similar, the time and energy required are usually much higher when you are involved in conflicts where the:

1. Emotions of the participants are at more elevated levels.
2. The perceived consequences are more significant.

With that being said, managing disagreements well requires awareness of your emotions and the impact of those emotions on your behavior and the behavior of others. When you are riding on an emotional roller coaster, it is likely that you:

1. Will not be in touch with your feelings.
2. Are overwhelmed by your feelings.

You may become so stressed that you can only pay attention to a limited number of emotions and/or you may not be able to understand your own needs. Consequently, it becomes more challenging to communicate with others and establish what's really troubling you. By peeling away the emotional onion, your ability to manage your emotions often depends on your ability to manage stress quickly while remaining alert and calm—and that takes practice. Once you have corralled your emotions, you can focus on behaviors that are more likely to help achieve positive outcomes. Besides self-awareness and managing emotions, other techniques for disagreeing well include:

1. **Focusing on the relationship**—Make the relationship a priority. Maintain and strengthen the relationship rather than *winning* the argument. When you demonstrate that winning is what's important, your behavior can be threatening, and you can expect the other person to demonstrate *fight-or-flight* behaviors. Practice being respectful of the other person and his or her viewpoint.

2. **Being aware of the other party's interests**—Develop and demonstrate a clear understanding of what is important to the other person (as was discussed in Chapter 4). You can then answer the important question: "What's in it for them?" while searching for solutions that may not be optimal from your perspective but provide benefits that are acceptable to the parties involved.

3. **Finding a willingness to address the issues**—Avoiding disagreements/conflicts requires judgment. Sometimes it is acceptable to let minor disagreements pass, or in other words, *pick your battles*. Consider whether the issue is really worth your time and energy, and then be willing to address disagreements/conflicts. When you enter a situation where you already feel threatened because of past experiences, it can be difficult to address issues in an appropriate, problem-solving way. Instead, you may either shut down or blow up in anger. In addition, you alert others, who may attempt to take advantage of less assertive people, when you show that you are uncomfortable addressing disagreements.

4. **Focusing on solving the problem**—Solving a problem that is inherent in a disagreement is of paramount importance, rather than arguing about who is right. It is important to fully understand the source of the disagreement before attempting to resolve it (i.e., address the problem, not the symptoms). Effective problem solving also includes evaluating alternative solutions and taking care to consider multiple interests and points of view. And, as

anyone who has ever experienced disagreement/conflict can attest, sometimes the chosen solution is unsuccessful. Individuals can use problem-solving skills by demonstrating a willingness to revisit unresolved issues and try another solution.

5. **Acknowledging the other person**—Acknowledge the other person's position, viewpoint, or solution. Appreciate their feelings by paraphrasing what they have said, which demonstrates that you understand their viewpoint. You do not have to agree, but show that you acknowledge their input.

6. **Being open to challenges**—Be open to people who are challenging you and practice how you can question their ideas and not them personally. Challenge ideas, concepts, and solutions, but avoid beliefs, culture, and motives.

7. **Searching for alternatives**—Rather than your position and their position, consider if there is an alternate position that is acceptable to everyone. (As an example, revisit the case study involving JoAnn and Percy in Section 5.9).

8. **Watching for the win–lose voice**—Beware of the boogieman of resolving disagreements who whispers in your ear subconsciously, "If you agree, you *lose*." When you listen, explore, and paraphrase, you are not signaling that you agree. The decision to agree or not comes *after* you listen. You can always state your position and call a timeout in order for the parties to consider other alternatives. A timeout is a viable option when parties are stuck in disagreements.

9. **Using the one-to-five-finger decision tool**—You will undoubtedly find yourself in situations where:
   - A team is having difficulty reaching a decision.
   - You want to close discussions and move on.
   - You need to confirm that you have consensus on actions or decisions.
   - You will have to help a team to move forward when they are stuck in discussions and appear to be unable to resolve differences.

A useful tool in these and other circumstances where teams are *stuck* in discussions and need to move forward is the one-to-five-finger decision tool that is shown in Table 8.1.

Table 8.1   One-to-five-finger decision tool

Sign	Meaning
1 Finger	Don't support, actively oppose
2 Fingers	On the fence, will go along
3 Fingers	Will support, with conditions
4 Fingers	Will support
5 Fingers	Committed, will try to convince others

To use the tool, simply ask the team a question:

- Are we ready to move on?
- Have we agreed to . . . ?
- Do we agree to take action to . . . ?
- Have we decided to . . . ?

After each question, ask the team to vote by holding up a finger representing their position. If everyone has three fingers or more, confirm and move on. When people hold up one or two fingers, take the time to resolve differences by asking those who voted with one or two fingers what it would take to convince them to vote with three or more fingers. You can then open discussions and work toward an acceptable solution.

We recommend *not* asking people why they voted with one or two fingers. They are likely to answer "because" (and give you their reasons). Others are likely to offer counterpoints to convince people to change their vote and the team ends up in a discussion of "because this" and "because that." Rather, everyone is accountable to help the team reach a decision. It is more constructive to ask people what would change their vote rather than trying to change the reasoning for their vote.

8.5   STRATEGIES FOR MANAGING DISAGREEMENTS/CONFLICTS

There are a number of strategies employed to resolve conflicts. They are mentioned here to provide context to your efforts to resolve disagreements.[4] The utility of any of these approaches is dependent on the behaviors listed in the previous section:

1. **Forcing or directing**—The strength or position of authority of one person dictates a solution. This approach has its place in situations where there is an eminent physical crisis. For example, a house is on fire and the first responders *order* people to evacuate, or in an operating room where the surgeon must make an immediate decision on a procedure. This approach, when employed outside of the situation of physical crisis, often leads to one party winning and the other losing because people do not have an opportunity to express their concerns. This can lead to bad feelings or poor implementation of the decision.

2. **Collaboration/problem solving**—Parties to the disagreement/conflict focus on solutions rather than positions. Prerequisites to this approach include trust/relationship among those involved, a focus on solving the problem rather than winning, and a willingness to explore alternatives. It does require emotional maturity and may require time and work to problem solve.

3. **Compromising/reconciling**—The parties bargain in the search for a solution and this may require both parties to give up something. This takes less time than collaboration but is likely to result in less commitment to the outcome because it is nobody's preferred option.

4. **Withdrawal/avoidance**—Participants retreat from the actual or potential disagreement and basically act as if there is no problem. This can be effective if those in conflict need time to cool down before any future discussions, or if the conflict is unimportant and will simply resolve itself, given time. However, this can lead to distrust, rework, and lost time, along with wasting considerable energy, if the issues go *underground* and fester only to later bloom into a considerable conflict.

5. **Smoothing/accommodating**—Participants de-emphasize the differences and emphasize common ground, thus avoiding the root causes of the disagreement. This can work in situations where the relationship is more important than the issue (e.g., customer/supplier situations). This strategy does not work when one party feels the conflict must be resolved.

The use of any of these strategies can be facilitated by either escalating the conflict to a person of higher authority or by seeking the assistance of a respected third party.

8.5.1   Escalation

Many people avoid escalating issues to people with more authority because of one or more of the following reasons:

1. Superiors want solutions, not problems.
2. The parties appear less competent because they cannot solve the problems on their own.
3. The person of authority may decide against the participants' positions.

Escalating to a person with more authority can be appropriate because:

1. Those in higher positions of authority may have a line of sight toward solutions that would not be thought of or available to those lower in the organization (e.g., budget money available).
2. Those in higher positions of authority may have a line of sight toward other activities that can be leveraged/used in the current situation.
3. Those in higher positions of authority may have a line of sight toward strategic imperatives that would favor one solution over another.

It is important that both parties participate or that both points of view are fairly represented when approaching people who have more authority. When escalating, do not ask someone to solve the problem, but rather show what has been considered and ask if there are other possible solutions.

8.5.2   Seeking Assistance from a Respected Third Party

This approach can be less intimidating than escalating to a superior and can keep the higher authority from having to force a solution. It can be helpful when:

1. The parties lack the subject matter expertise/experience to envision creative alternatives outside of the solutions preferred by either party.
2. The parties recognize that they are emotionally attached to their preferred solution and need to seek an objective viewpoint.
3. The parties actually look for coaching on their approach/process for solving the conflict.

8.6   CHECKLIST FOR RESPONSES TO DISAGREEMENTS

Table 8.2 categorizes many of the behaviors that can support or undermine effective responses to disagreements. As you experience disagreements in your personal and/or work lives, consider where you are on the behavior list shown in Table 8.2 and recalibrate your behaviors when appropriate.

Table 8.2   Behavioral responses to disagreements

Effective Behaviors in Response to Disagreements	Ineffective Responses to Disagreements; Behaviors to Avoid
I pause and try to understand another person's viewpoint during disagreements.	I often focus on my needs during disagreements and fail to recognize and/or address what is important to others.
I can remain calm and respectful when another person becomes emotional.	I can get emotional, angry, or aggressive during disagreements.
I can move past disagreements without becoming resentful or withdrawing.	I can be resentful and/or withdraw from relationships after disagreements.
I can focus on solving problems/ underlying causes during disagreements.	I argue for my position during disagreements and find it difficult to collaborate/problem-solve.
I prefer to address disagreements quickly and not let them linger.	I avoid disagreements fearing a bad outcome, damage to relationships, or emotional outbreaks.

The following case study describes an example of a workplace disagreement.

CASE STUDY ON RESOLVING DISAGREEMENTS

John recently found out that he is being considered for a promotion to be the team leader of the IT support group. In addition, John has heard that a fellow employee, Jason, has not been contributing as much as he has in the past toward completing the normal weekly work of the team. Jason claims he is swamped with work and is going through the emotional aftermath of a bitter divorce. Some fellow workers are

(continues)

voicing concerns that Jason's work has really fallen off and that it is impacting their ability to meet their work commitments. Jason's fellow workers want to take their complaint to the department manager.

John is a good friend of Jason's and knows that Jason is capable, but John feels that Jason is overdramatizing his problems. As the potential new team leader, John feels a need to address the situation. Consequently, at an offsite lunch with Jason, John takes the opportunity to voice his concerns in a straightforward manner. Jason gets defensive, maintaining that he has been meeting his work commitments, and accuses John of not sympathizing or understanding his situation.

As Jason's friend, and potential new team leader, what would you do if you were John in this situation? Let's look at this case example from several different perspectives.

8.6.1 Feedback

The four *hot buttons* listed here were previously presented in Chapter 5. Let's apply them to the case study involving Jason and John:

1. **False**—Could Jason have rejected the feedback because he *believed* it was not true?
2. **Invalid feedback**—John is a friend of Jason's; could Jason have focused on *who* was giving the feedback rather than the feedback itself? John is not currently the team leader; did Jason feel John was not qualified to give him feedback?
3. **Self-concept**—If Jason considers himself a good and reliable team member (his self-concept), could the feedback have been rejected because it challenged his self-concept?
4. **Wrong person**—In this instance, Jason did not ask for feedback. The feedback that was given was unsolicited. There is no indication in the case study that John asked permission to give feedback. In addition, John did not ask Jason to evaluate his own performance. Given Jason's situation, if John had asked Jason to perform a self-assessment, it might have provided insights into how to frame the feedback, such as being more supportive rather than pointing out his lack of performance.

The case study states that John brought up his concerns in a straightforward manner. If this means John stated that Jason's work output was not meeting expectations (an evaluation) and it is impacting the team's performance (an evaluation), it is possible that the feedback touched all four of these buttons, and Jason's defensive reaction would be expected. Furthermore, it is likely that Jason is aware that his performance is declining or has declined.

John already has a relationship with Jason. Knowing he's going through a bitter divorce, there may have been an opportunity to talk to Jason sooner and offer the support that he may have needed (continue building the relationship before a problem arose). You could argue that Jason's divorce was a personal matter and not John's business. However, not addressing Jason's performance is an avoidance strategy, and not ideal in this situation. Jason's lack of performance is impacting the performance of the team. It is likely that the situation will go underground only to appear later, requiring more time to resolve.

8.6.2 Feeling/Emotional State

1. Your feelings about this situation:
   - If you were John and allowed, or encouraged, other team members to escalate Jason's lack of performance to the manager, how would you feel? Did you let your friend down?
   - If this situation was escalated to the department manager, would this reflect poorly on your leadership and potential promotion because you did not address the issue with Jason's performance?
2. Jason's feelings:
   - We can assume Jason's level of stress is elevated due to the divorce and his work would be impacted.
   - In addition, it is likely that Jason is aware that his performance has declined, which would add to his level of stress and impact his performance.

8.6.3 This Is What We Know

1. John is Jason's friend.
2. Jason has been a good worker and has met work expectations in the past.
3. Jason's recent performance has not met expectations.

8.6.4 We Can Make Some Assumptions

1. Jason is stressed over his divorce (finances, custody of children, guilt, etc.).

2. Jason is stressed over his decline in work output.
3. John may have spoken to Jason as a potential team leader to demonstrate his leadership strength rather than to support Jason in the short term. A straightforward evaluation of performance may have added to Jason's stress, eliciting an emotional response to John's feedback.

If we back up a bit, rather than confronting Jason about his performance in a straightforward way, it may have been better to first ask Jason how he feels about work, his divorce, etc., thereby focusing on the relationship rather than the work output in the short term. Recall the discussion in Section 5.7 about asking the receiver of feedback to self-assess before providing your feedback. Assuming that Jason expresses his feelings, then John could:

1. Ask Jason for suggestions
2. Offload some work to other team members in the short term
3. Arrange for time off for Jason and bring in another person from another team to help with the workload

Going forward at this point, there are several opportunities:

1. Meet with Jason again and talk about how you feel about the lunch meeting and own your role in how that meeting ended.
2. Ask Jason how he felt about the previous meeting; listen to understand and clarify feelings. Confirm Jason's past performance and empathize about the difficulty of the divorce (focus on your relationship with Jason).
3. Use active listening to have a conversation about work, and brainstorm with Jason about how to move forward:
   - Get someone from another team to help out in the short term.
   - Seek assistance from the HR organization (e.g., an Employee Assistance Program) to support Jason through his divorce (assuming Jason agrees).
   - Arrange for time off for Jason to work through his personal situation.
   - Alert your supervisor to the situation and the actions you are taking. Assure that you have his/her support and be open to other suggestions the supervisor may have.
   - Set a realistic time frame for Jason to bring his performance up to expectations. Setting that time frame may not be feasible until some of the other suggestions have been attempted.

8.7   FOCUS AREA UPDATE FOR DISAGREEING WELL

Do you have additional insights about disagreeing well based on the material in Section 8.3 (*When Should You Resolve Disagreements*), 8.4 (*What Can You Do to Manage Disagreements/Conflicts*), 8.5 (*Strategies for Managing Disagreements/Conflicts*), or 8.6 (*Checklist for Responses to Disagreements*)? If so, take the opportunity, as you have done in previous chapters, to update your focus areas about behaviors that will build your ability to disagree well.

FINAL FOCUS AREAS FOR CHAPTER 8

Focus area 1—Describe a behavior that would improve your ability to disagree well and mine value from disagreements (e.g., when I listen to understand, it doesn't mean I agree with another's position):

_____

_____

Focus area 2—Describe a behavior that would improve your ability to disagree well and mine value from disagreements:

_____

_____

Don't forget to update the template you downloaded from www.jrosspub.com/CLT to keep track of your focus areas created in exercises throughout this book.

8.8   KEY TAKEAWAYS

The key takeaways from this chapter include:

1. Disagreements can be trivial or significant and, in either case, the sooner that differences are resolved, the probability of a satisfactory resolution increases.
2. Building relationships/trust before they are needed is an important strategy for successful resolution of disagreements.

3. There are a number of behaviors to develop that increase the probability of successfully resolving disagreements/conflicts.
4. There are a number of strategies that can be employed to solve conflict, and the success of these strategies is largely dependent on the behaviors presented in this chapter.
5. There is a checklist of healthy and unhealthy responses to disagreements/conflict.
6. Be open to being challenged and appropriately challenging others.
7. You have updated focus areas regarding your behaviors that support disagreeing well.

ENDNOTES

1. Benjamin, Kimberly. 2021. "6 Steps to Conflict Resolution in the Workplace." Retrieved May 21, 2021, from *HR Daily Advisor* at https://hrdailyadvisor.blr.com/2013/06/24/6-steps-to-conflict-resolution-in-the-workplace/.
2. Marter, Joyce. 2017. "10 Tips for Resolving Conflict." Retrieved May 3, 2021, from the *HuffPost* at https://www.huffpost.com/entry/conscious-relationships_b_4504510.
3. Forbes Coaches Council. 2017. "11 Ways You Can Better Resolve Conflicts." Retrieved June 4, 2021, from *Forbes* at https://www.forbes.com/sites/forbescoachescouncil/2017/11/14/11-ways-you-can-better-handle-conflict-resolution/?sh=5cc209b82854.
4. Project Management Institute. 2017. *A Guide to the Project Management Body of Knowledge.* Sixth Edition. Newtown Square, PA. pp. 348–349.

CHAPTER 9

PRESENTING IS LEADING

"The success of your presentation will be judged not by the knowledge you send but by what the listener receives."

—Lilly Walters (keynote speaker)

CHAPTER ROADMAP

Presentation skills are an important component of a leader's communication tool set. You may need to present an idea, propose a solution, provide an overview of a project, deliver a key message, persuade constituents, inspire a team, and much more. This chapter focuses on your development of presentation skills. The following list describes the roadmap we will follow in this chapter:

1. Opening exercise
2. Know your constituents
3. Know your message
4. Do your research
5. Organize your presentation
6. Overcome anxiety
7. Deliver
8. Key takeaways
9. Your assignment
10. Update your communications transformation focus areas

9.1 OPENING EXERCISE

For your opening exercise, take the initiative to analyze a minimum of two presentations you have heard. The presentations can be of any length and can be live presentations or recorded presentations (with video). We will keep the analysis simple. For each of the two presentations, ask the following five questions and document your findings:

1. What was the purpose of the presentation?

    - Presentation 1: _____

    - Presentation 2: _____

2. Was the presentation effective? Did it make you think, act, or feel differently?

    - Presentation 1: _____

    - Presentation 2: _____

3. Did the speaker keep you engaged? How?

    - Presentation 1: _____

    - Presentation 2: _____

4. What did the speaker do well?

    - Presentation 1: _____

    - Presentation 2: _____

5. What could the speaker have done to improve the presentation?

    - Presentation 1: _____

    - Presentation 2: _____

Refer to your answers and keep those two presentations in mind as we progress through the lessons in this chapter.

Before we proceed further, did you notice the word *constituents* in item 2 in the roadmap of this chapter? You are going to see that term throughout this chapter and again in Chapter 14. Why "constituents" and not just the term "audience," particularly in discussing presentations and leadership? Here is why.

CONSTITUENTS GET TO VOTE

People will choose (e.g., vote) on whether to respond to a leader's request whether that request is in person or in another form of communication. They can express that vote verbally or more frequently in their behavior. They may ignore the request, comply (give the minimum effort), or commit (devote the time and energy needed to fulfill the leader's request). As an example, consider the request by many world leaders for their constituents to respond to the COVID-19 pandemic by wearing masks, using social distancing, and obtaining the regimen of vaccines:

1. Some people refused their leader's request even in the face of health and economic hardships.
2. Many people complied and did the minimum by wearing masks in some situations but not in others, made an effort to obtain a vaccine when it was convenient, and paid some attention to social distancing in public places but not with friends within their homes.
3. Many more people committed and wore masks whenever they were in contact with others, carried extra masks and offered masks to those without them, received the regimen of vaccines as soon as they were made available, encouraged others to get vaccinated, and practiced social distancing.

As a leader, do not assume people will follow. Develop a mindset that your audience, whether one person, your project team, a room full of peers, or a whole country, will vote whether to follow. Consider your audience as your constituents.

9.2   KNOW YOUR CONSTITUENTS

To become a more powerful presenter, you must first get to know your constituents. Whether you have one constituent or many, do you know their expectations? Do you know what motivates them? If you have many constituents, are there some common interests? What's on their minds? The success of your presentation is determined by your constituents, not by you.

Why should you invest your time understanding your constituents? Rob Sherman, in the introduction to his book *Sherman's 21 Laws of Speaking*, writes that "One executive observed, just five minutes in front of the right audience can be worth more than a whole year behind your desk."[1]

Brian Tracy, in his book *Speak to Win: How to Present with Power in Any Situation*, states that "The starting point of preparation is your audience. Remember, it is not about you; it is about them."[2] In preparing your presentation, ask yourself:

- "Why do my constituents need this presentation?"
- "Why am I the one making this presentation?"
- "Why is it important for my message to be heard?"

It is important that you invest the time to get to know your audience. The following list includes some basic questions to use in your analysis:

1. How much influence or power do your constituents possess? Are you presenting to a group of executives? Will you be presenting to professionals? Will the audience be mixed (individuals with varying levels of influence)?
2. What are the specific interests of your constituents?
3. What are the individual roles and responsibilities of your constituents?
4. Are there any significant events occurring in the organization that could affect the perspectives of your constituents?
5. What are the demographics (ages, income levels, education, occupations, gender, etc.) of your constituents and how should you consider these in your presentation?
6. Are there any *controversial subjects* that should be avoided? If so, be prepared to handle these if they come up or surface as questions.
7. Conversely, are there any *burning questions* that should be addressed? If so, do your homework and determine the best way to handle these prior to the presentation.

To get the answers to these questions, consider interviewing the constituents prior to the presentation. If you are unable to interview the constituents, interview others who might have knowledge of the constituents or answers to the questions that were previously identified. By answering these questions and adjusting your presentation accordingly, you will be better prepared and will set yourself up for a successful presentation. This analysis may also determine whether or not you should conduct multiple presentations to address diverse constituents.

9.3   KNOW YOUR MESSAGE

Your message should be clear and simple. You should be able to write your message in a one sentence headline or phrase. One simple technique for clarifying your message before you give your presentation is to write it on a three-by-five-inch index card, thus making your message as concise as possible. The simpler the message, the more powerful it will be.

If you have mixed messages or multiple important messages, you should consider separate presentations. Once you settle on your message, you then have the foundation for your presentation.

Craig Valentine, a former Toastmasters World Champion of Public Speaking, says that "Without the foundational message, it is like you are building a castle on quicksand."

In developing your message, you should also consider the purpose of your presentation. Ask yourself, "Why are you giving this presentation?" More specifically, "Why are you giving this presentation to these constituents at this point in time? What is the purpose for your presentation?" Every planned presentation should have a general and a specific purpose (see Table 9.1). You can use the following table to define your purpose and refine your message more specifically.

Table 9.1   Determining general and specific purposes

General Purpose	Specific Purpose Questions
Inform	Why do the constituents need this information? Are these the right constituents? What specific information is important to the constituents? What should the constituents do with this information?
Persuade	Why do the constituents need to be persuaded? What specifically are you promoting? Is there a specific action expected of the constituents? Are the points clear and actionable? Will the constituents be given factual and emotional reasons to take action? Will there be a clear call to action?
Inspire	Why inspire the constituents? Why is it important that the constituents be inspired? What is the value of this presentation to the constituents?
Entertain	Why should the constituents be entertained? Even with an entertaining speech, there should be a *why* behind the entertainment—even if the why is just to provide an entertainment break. Entertaining is often combined with one of the other purposes to make the other purposes more effective.

Once you have defined your message, you can then build your presentation around it. Your message becomes your content filter and editor. All research, supporting material, stories, and content should support and enhance your message. As you develop your material, use your defined message to determine if your material supports the point or not. If it doesn't support your point, it doesn't belong in your presentation.

More often than not, your presentation and the message surrounding it will involve some *call to action* for the receivers of your presentation. Your call to action could be to approve a vision, invest in a project, sign a contract, commit to a plan, or any number of actions. Your message should be clear and strong enough to ensure that when you finish your presentation, your audience will get the message and will know what is expected of them.

If you are using presentation software or slides, focus on keeping the slides simple and clear. Avoid cluttering the slides with too many details. You can always supplement the primary presentation with reading material that contains any necessary detail.

9.4   DO YOUR RESEARCH

"To be great up there . . . prepare four times the amount of material and research you will need."[3]

—Lilly Walters

Prepare for your presentations by researching appropriately because your credibility could be at stake. Whether your presentation is a one-minute elevator speech or a one-hour technical presentation, invest the time to research your topic. Proper research will enhance your presentation power and you will gain valuable credibility.

Once you have determined your message and both the general and specific purposes for your presentation, collect your material and research to support your message. Support material can include any of the following:

1. **Stories and anecdotes** (personal and referred)—Stories and anecdotes appeal to the emotions and can be highly effective in persuading or requesting a call to action.

2. **Statistics and metrics**—These can come from the industry, credible information sources, the company, or any other relevant source.
3. **Facts**—Separate fact from fiction and emotion. Use relevant facts to support your points. Any historical information related to your topic can be useful.
4. **Quotes**—Find relevant quotes to support your message. Quotes add power to your speech and demonstrate that you have researched your presentation.
5. **Testimony**—A relevant testimony, or testimonies, can also add power to your presentation and can be used to make a point. Testimony differs from quotes in that testimony typically is a firsthand experience.
6. **Examples**—Examples can be used to clarify concepts.
7. **Metaphors**—Metaphors can be used to simplify difficult concepts, proposals, or ideas.
8. **Visual aids**—Visual aids, if used properly, can also be highly effective in presenting difficult concepts.

Once you have collected your material and conducted your research, use your strongest material to support your points. The challenge of detailed information and material is to find ways to present it so that it is understandable by your audience and *connects* with them. That is why it is so important to know to whom you are presenting. Your research and material may have to be slanted differently, depending on the technical knowledge of your audience.

You should also cross-check your facts and sources, especially when you have obtained material from the internet. One bad fact or misrepresented statistic can damage your credibility and diminish the power of your presentation.

9.5   ORGANIZE YOUR PRESENTATION

Organize your material to support your message to ensure that you have given your audience a roadmap—a path to understanding and accepting your message. Every presentation should have a clearly defined opening, middle (the body of the speech), and a close:

1. **Outlining**—You should outline your presentation by beginning with your clearly defined message, and then by defining the

individual supporting points for your presentation. Once you have your points, you can then organize your supporting material around these points. Your outline should also consider the ordering of your major points. Will you present your points chronologically or does some other order make more sense? There is no right way or wrong way. You should organize it in a way that helps you create a stronger presentation.

2. **The opening**—The opening, or introduction, of your presentation is your opportunity to connect with your audience. You could start with an anecdote, a joke, a story, or a startling fact or question. But however you open your presentation, it should be relevant to your message and your presentation. Your opening should be attention-getting and introduce your message, either directly or indirectly. It should let your audience know what you are thinking. A good practice is to write out the introduction word for word to ensure that it is as effective as possible.

3. **The middle (body)**—The middle, or body, of the speech will contain the majority of your material and your primary supporting points for your message. This is where you organize your material around your key points. Each point should be clearly defined and supported by your research material and/or stories. The number of points you wish to make will, of course, be determined by the amount of time you have available. For a short speech or presentation, however, three to five points is usually more than enough to deliver your message. Generally, simple is more effective than complex.

4. **The close**—The close of your presentation is your opportunity to finalize your message and state your call to action, either directly or indirectly. The close is also your opportunity to recap your main points and hammer home your message. Brian Tracy states that "The best strategy for ending with a bang is to plan your close before you plan the rest of your speech." A strong close will not only make your presentation memorable, but it will establish a rapport with your audience, thereby enhancing your relationships and setting up positive expectations for your future presentations.

9.6   OVERCOMING ANXIETY

". . . people's well-documented nervousness, with regard to public speaking, derives from what Carl Jung concluded was the hard-wired mother of all fears: fear of the unknown." [4]

—Tony Jeary

Anxiety is natural and nerve-racking but can also be used to your benefit. Leaders with more than adequate knowledge, skills, and perspectives may fall victim to the *beast* of anxiety during a critical presentation. The beast is one of our basic human emotions. It is so strong that it can significantly change the intent of the presenter's objectives. The beast is fear.

Training on presentation skills is not complete without a focus on overcoming anxiety or fear. Overcoming the beast is essential to not only providing an effective presentation but also to becoming an effective leader and communicator.

So, how do we minimize our fear of the unknown? Make more of the unknown become known. This translates into simple strategies, such as:

1. **Understand the fear**—This strategy is as simple as understanding what it is that you fear about giving your presentation. A simple analysis often proves to you that your greatest fears have no foundation. One common fear, for example, is the fear that you will make errors in your presentation. So what? No one is perfect. If you have an important message, the biggest error of all is to not give the presentation! Understand your fear and you will most likely find that there is no basis for it.

2. **Research your audience**—As discussed earlier in this chapter, if you understand your audience, you will connect with them. Connecting with your audience will help you overcome anxiety.

3. **Research your topic**—Become comfortable with your material and research your topic so that you become the expert, if only temporarily. This also helps reduce the unknowns.

4. **Visualize**—Ruben Gonzalez, a former Olympic athlete and professional speaker, once said, "Your mind does not know the difference between reality and fantasy." If you take the effort to visualize and mentally rehearse your presentation, your mind will

remember the live presentation as something you've done before, thereby reducing your anxiety and making your presentation more professional and polished.

5. **Remember the message**—Since you have an important message (obviously, or you wouldn't be giving it), remember how important that message is to your audience. What key questions are you addressing? How important is your message to them? If you don't give your constituents this message, what is the negative impact? Remembering the importance of your message will give you strength and help you overcome any fears you may have.

6. **Preparation**—The beast will have a difficult time dealing with a prepared presenter. Preparation begins with the basics. Know your audience. What should you do to prepare for them? What type of presentation are these people expecting? Do they expect information at a generic level or at a detailed level? Know your *stage*: will you be giving your presentation in a meeting room for six people, a boardroom, or from a lectern in a darkened auditorium in front of several hundred people with a spotlight on you? Will you be using a microphone? Will you be competing with distractions or food and drink? The list can go on and on, but the more you can ask and answer these questions for yourself, the better prepared you will be. Know your material and understand your topic. This does not mean memorizing your presentation word for word, but it does mean knowing it well enough that you can recover from any distraction.

7. **Mentally rehearse**—Rehearse until you become comfortable with your presentation. Eliminate your own negative surprises.

8. **Use notes**—It's okay to use notes. Notes may reduce your anxiety and help you with the flow of your presentation. Many effective speakers use notes, so use them when you rehearse so that they don't become distractions when you give the live presentation.

9.7 DELIVER

Even if you have great content and a critical message, poor delivery will lessen the power of your message and your content. On the other hand, weaker content can be enhanced with great delivery. You should, of course, strive for both powerful content *and* delivery. The great news about delivery is that it can be improved through practice. Delivery includes the following components:

1. **Body language**—The key to effective body language is to know what messages your body language and gestures communicate to the audience. You should strive to eliminate any bad habits (swaying, jingling change, hands in pockets, etc.) and become purposeful in all of your movements and hand gestures.

2. **Eye contact**—Use eye contact to connect with your audience and establish it before you start speaking. By starting with eye contact, you build a rapport with the audience. If your audience is large, scan the entire room, then connect with different individuals to make your presentation more engaging.

3. **Vocal variety**—Strive to control the use of your voice to vary your delivery of the message. Move from monotone to varied speeds, pitches, and volume. Record your presentations and review them for your use of vocal variety.

4. **Pauses**—Use pauses to effectively punctuate your speech and highlight key points. Sometimes, the most powerful thing you can do during a speech or presentation is to not speak.

5. **Language**—Use of carefully selected words to paint an image or tell a story can add significantly to the power and effectiveness of your presentation. Speakers should select words that appeal to all the senses.

A TRUE STORY

Larry was an effective project manager in a healthcare organization; he always met the goals of his assigned projects. His team members respected him, and he engaged his stakeholders effectively, often receiving rave reviews for his performance as a project manager. Although his communication skills were effective, he tended to get hung up on the details during his presentations to executives.

While he was leading a key strategic project, he was asked to provide an update to an executive committee in the organization. During the presentation, he came across as nervous and unprepared. He also provided much more detail than was required or expected by that committee.

After the presentation, one of the executives approached Larry's manager and asked, "Why was he assigned to this project as a project manager? He does not seem qualified to lead this important project." Ouch!

(continues)

Make no mistake, the quality of your presentation can reflect on your perceived leadership ability.

To continue with this story, Larry's manager decided to personally coach Larry with his next presentation to the same committee. Larry was willing to be coached and he prepared diligently. He simplified his content, focusing on the key points. He prepared for the hard questions and learned (through rehearsal) to stay away from details unless it was relevant to a specific question. With help from his manager and others, Larry learned to adapt his mindset to those on the executive committee.

After the next presentation, the same executive approached Larry's manager again and said, "I understand now why he is the project manager for this key project. He's great!"

9.8 FOCUS AREA UPDATE FOR PRESENTING IS LEADING

As you recall the lessons in this chapter, do you have additional insights regarding your presentation skills? Consider the following as you think about your focus areas for improvement:

1. Apply the presentation strategies that were discussed in this chapter. Focus on an upcoming presentation opportunity and prepare using the following guidelines:
   - Clearly define your message and purpose. Write them down and use them to steer your preparation and delivery.
   - Analyze your audience for this upcoming presentation opportunity. How will you consider the audience's needs and expectations in your presentation?
   - Be clear where and how you will be giving the presentation and prepare appropriately.
   - Outline your presentation. For a shorter presentation (less than 10 minutes), you might consider writing it.
   - If you will be using visual aids or a presentation tool (e.g., PowerPoint or Pages), develop your visual presentation.
   - Rehearse your presentation until you feel comfortable and confident.
   - Give your presentation (record it if possible and appropriate).
   - Seek feedback from your audience members (if appropriate).

- Ask someone you trust to observe your presentation and provide you with feedback (pros and cons).

2. Now, list your behavior-based focus areas, taking into consideration the insights gained from the material in this chapter. What two focus areas would improve your presentation skills?

FOCUS AREAS FOR CHAPTER 9

Focus area 1—Describe a behavior to help you improve your presentation skills (e.g., I want to invest more time on my critical presentation up front to define the message and ensure everything in my presentation supports that message):

_____

_____

Focus area 2—Describe a behavior to help you improve your presentation skills:

_____

_____

Don't forget to update the template you downloaded from www.jross pub.com/CLT to keep track of your focus areas created in exercises throughout this book.

9.9   SELECTING YOUR HIGHEST PRIORITY COMMUNICATION FOCUS AREAS

Congratulations! We have now completed the communications section of this book and it is time to prioritize and select your highest priority communication focus areas.

Whether you inventoried your chapter focus areas in the template found at www.jrosspub.com/CLT, in the book, or used some other method, take time now to review those focus areas. Keep in mind as you complete your review that you will be asked to prioritize your communication focus areas and choose no more than three to carry forward at this point in time. Here is a rundown of key points from each of the communication chapters in this book:

1. Chapter 2: Failing to Communicate Is Not an Option
   - Established a baseline of your communication process skills that may be used to clarify opportunities for improved behavior-based skills in later chapters
2. Chapter 3: Who Are You? Your Personality Traits
   - Completed the Insight Inventory® personality profile and found your personality traits
   - Identified your preferred behaviors among those personality traits
   - Learned how you can interact with dissimilar preferences
   - Listed your initial set of behavior-based focus areas
3. Chapter 4: Listen Better to Succeed
   - Learned the benefits of improved listening and questioning
   - Learned tools and techniques to improve listening skills
   - Listed your behaviors/habits that get in the way of listening
   - Listed your behavior-based focus areas
4. Chapter 5: Receiving and Giving Feedback—Are You Ready?
   - We can learn from feedback, whether it is wrong, inappropriately given, or hurtful in some way
   - Reasons we reject feedback
   - Types of feedback and how to bring clarity to feedback you receive
   - When and how to reject feedback
   - Guides for giving feedback
   - Three modes of giving feedback
   - Challenging performance evaluations
   - Listed your behavior-based focus areas
5. Chapter 6: Every Relationship Has Value
   - Your experiences with relationships
   - Relationships exist to satisfy a need
   - Build relationships before you need them
   - Tools and techniques for building relationships
   - Listed your behavior-based focus areas
6. Chapter 7: Consequential Communication
   - Assessing the context of a critical conversation (e.g., situation, participants, and outcomes)

- Planning the conversation
- Executing the conversation
- Closing the conversation
- Listed your behavior-based focus areas

7. Chapter 8: Mining Disagreements for Value
   - Types of disagreements
   - Your experience with disagreements
   - When to address disagreements
   - Tools and techniques for disagreeing well
   - Listed your behavior-based focus areas

8. Chapter 9: Presenting Is Leading
   - Purpose: what is the audience listening for?
   - Develop the presentation; do your research
   - Organize the presentation (opening, body, and close)
   - Deliver the presentation
   - Respond to questions
   - Listed your behavior-based focus areas

Take time now to prioritize your list of communication focus areas. Consider the following criteria when choosing your highest priority communication focus areas:

1. Positive impact on your work and/or personal life (high impact is preferable)
2. Time to achieve measurable results (shorter time to achieve results is preferable)
3. Difficulty in achieving results (the more difficult to achieve results, the more time and effort is required)
4. Level of your commitment (high level of personal commitment is essential)

There is a tool provided in Appendix C for those readers who prefer a more rigorous methodology for selecting the highest priority focus areas.

Now, list your *three* highest priority communication focus areas on the next page. We suggest no more than three because of existing commitments and demands on your time. Don't forget to update your downloaded template as well.

YOUR FINAL HIGH-PRIORITY FOCUS AREAS TO IMPROVE YOUR COMMUNICATION SKILLS

Communication high-priority focus area 1—

_____

_____

Communication high-priority focus area 2—

_____

_____

Communication high-priority focus area 3—

_____

_____

9.10   KEY TAKEAWAYS

The key takeaways for this chapter include the following:

1. Presentations can enhance your communications and raise your credibility.
2. Know your constituents/audience well enough to establish a common connection through your presentations.
3. Own your message. Your message should be clear and easy to understand.
4. Research as if your professional life depends on it (because it does!).
5. Organize your presentation to make it easy to follow.
6. Do not allow the beast of fear and anxiety to interfere with your message.
7. Develop and rehearse your delivery.
8. Make every presentation count.
9. Capture focus areas for improving presentation skills.

10. Confirm and prioritize behavior-based focus areas for Part I: Communication.

ENDNOTES

1. Sherman, R. 2005. *Sherman's 21 Laws of Speaking.* Blacklick, OH. Cedar Creek Press. p. 8.
2. Tracy, B. 2008. *Speak to Win: How to Present with Power in Any Situation.* New York, NY. AMACOM, a division of American Management Association. p. 19.
3. Walters, L. 2000. *Secrets of Superstar Speakers.* New York, NY. McGraw-Hill. p. 204.
4. Jeary, T. 2005. *Life Is a Series of Presentations.* New York, NY. Fireside. p. 132.

Part II

Leadership

CHAPTER 10

LEAD TO SUCCEED

"Great leaders are almost always great simplifiers, who can cut through argument, debate, and doubt to offer a solution everybody can understand."

—Colin Powell

CHAPTER ROADMAP

Everyone knows the names of those who have had a title *and* were great leaders—U.S. President Abraham Lincoln and UK Prime Minister Winston Churchill come to mind. And many of us have seen leaders who carry no title, but inspire others to follow, such as the young child in the park who organizes other children into a game on the spur of the moment, or the member of a work team who speaks of a future that galvanizes others to pursue. Martin Luther King identified a leader in this way: "A genuine leader is not a searcher for consensus but a molder of consensus." So, how do leaders mold consensus and find others to commit to them if they lack a title? That question is the focus of this chapter. More precisely, the goals of this chapter are first, to align on the concept of what leadership *is*; second, to recognize that it is a learned behavior; and finally, to agree on what leadership *is not*.

To achieve these goals, the chapter leverages the excellent work by the Gallup Organization in exploring the concepts of what leaders say they do. Next, it examines what those who follow leaders say they look for in a leader. Later in this chapter you will identify your behavior-based leadership focus areas, much like you have done with communication in Part I. The roadmap for this chapter includes:

1. Align on what leadership is and is not
2. Use your experiences with leadership to list focus areas based on those experiences

3. Complete an online self-assessment of your leadership skills
4. Explore what leaders do
5. Understand what people expect of leaders
6. Review leadership in the virtual environment
7. Confirm key behavior-based focus areas that will assist you in your journey to become an effective leader
8. Key takeaways

Throughout Part II, you will have the opportunity to add to, or modify, your behavior-based leadership focus areas.

10.1   WHAT LEADERSHIP IS—THE BASICS

There is a plethora of business literature documenting the differences between a leader and a manager.[1] Some of the adjectives that are traditionally applied to leaders and managers are listed in Table 10.1. While these distinctions occupy space in leadership literature, they really provide little value in truly understanding leaders and leadership. In addition, telling a manager that he/she is not people-oriented would likely lead to an uncomfortable conversation and a request to provide data to substantiate the assertion.

In reality, leaders often move between these two columns. Warren Bennis captured this distinction when he said, "Leadership is the capacity to translate vision into reality." Said another way, leaders reach for the future but are accountable for results today.

When the layers of the onion are peeled away on the concept of leadership, there is often an underlying assumption that the *leader* has been

Table 10.1   Focus of leaders and managers

Leader	Manager
Defines purpose	Defines tasks
Leads change	Focuses on results
Takes risks	Controls risks
Long-term	Short-term
Builds relationships	Builds systems and processes
Coaches	Directs
Motivates	Approves
People-oriented	Work-oriented

bestowed that position based on his or her title. Consequently, there is an expectation that the person who will lead is a *C-level* manager in an organization (a CEO), the team leader on a project, the president of the neighborhood association, or the chairperson of this year's charity gala, to name a few.

In this book we do away with that *position bias* in discussing leadership. Practically everyone has the opportunity and/or potential to be a leader, such as:

1. The building maintenance person who finds a more efficient way to clean a building
2. The project team member who envisions a way to capture more value for the organization on an existing project
3. The member of one family, in a team of two families planning a wedding, who helps the families resolve a difference of opinion on where the wedding should be held
4. The child at recess who has his/her friends involved in organizing the balls for games

In your work and personal life, there are opportunities for you to lead. Consequently, the definition of leadership followed in this book is:

*Leadership is the **art** of helping both the leader and others **move** toward **achieving** a **goal/aspiration**.*

The four key words in that definition are highlighted here:

1. **Art**—Although science, methodologies, skills, knowledge, and tools are associated with leadership, the application of these enablers requires wisdom to adapt them to current circumstances. That wisdom cannot be reduced to an equation. It is creatively applying these concepts to the canvas of realities in order to produce results.
2. **Move**—Would you want to be on a team that is moving forward, showing progress, and where results are apparent; or on a team that is stuck, involved in endless discussions and debates, and where results are invisible? Most of us would prefer the former. This situation creates its own energy and energizes people on the team to commit to the journey.
3. **Achieving**—Making progress is critical to the role of leadership. However, ultimately, achieving specific results that are tied to long-term goals follows the definition of leadership. As Peter

Drucker wisely stated, "Effective leadership is not about making speeches or being liked; leadership is defined by results, not attributes."

4. **Goal/aspiration**—The leader defines or helps the team decide where the team is going (aka the goal). In 1961 when John F. Kennedy stated, "I believe that this nation should commit itself to achieving the goal, before this decade is out, of landing a man on the moon and returning him safely to Earth," he energized the nation to do what seemed impossible at the time. In July of 1969, Neil Armstrong walked on the moon and returned safely to Earth.

To further refine your thoughts about leadership, let's leverage your experiences with it. When you think about leadership, what thoughts come to mind? An online search of the term *leadership* results in a plethora of approaches to define the actual concept of leadership, such as:

1. Styles of leadership: pragmatist, diplomat, steward, and idealist[2]
2. What leaders do: creative vision, inspire, motivate, etc.[3]
3. Leadership skills: empathy, team building, problem-solving, strategic thinking, etc.[4]

Notwithstanding the numerous views about leadership listed here, think about your experiences with leaders. In the space provided, list two impactful experiences that you have had with people whom you consider to be leaders, regardless of their title. Consider the following hallmarks of leaders as you list your experiences:

1. You trusted the leader and were willing to pursue their aspiration
2. It was clear to you where the leader was going, and achieving the goal met your needs
3. The leader supported your efforts and recognized your contributions
4. Results were achieved
5. The leader demonstrated the behaviors that were expected of you

Experience 1—Describe an experience with a leader that was impactful for you (e.g., you would follow them, commit to their vision, listen to them, they inspired you):

_____

_____

_____

Experience 2—Describe an experience with a leader that was impactful for you (e.g., you would follow them, commit to their vision, listen to them, they inspired you):

_____

_____

_____

Now think of two situations involving a leader that were not impactful for you or were impactful in a negative sense. Consider the following points when describing your experiences:

1. You did not _trust_ the leader or their message
2. The leader did not consider your needs or the needs of others when pursuing a goal
3. Results were not achieved
4. Your interactions with the leader were negative in the sense that:
   - There was a lack of understanding
   - The conversations were one way, and there was a lack of meaningful dialogue or debate of the issues
   - You were given direction rather than collaboration
   - There was a lack of support

Experience 1—Describe an experience with a leader that was not impactful for you:

_____

_____

_____

Experience 2—Describe an experience with a leader that was not impactful for you:

_____

_____

_____

Are there any behaviors that jump out from the preceding analyses? Behaviors these leaders should have done more of, less of, start doing, or stop doing? Leverage these experiences and list no more than three focus areas where you want to change your behavior in order to improve as a leader:

Focus area 1—Describe a behavior that would improve your leadership skills (e.g., ensure people understand our team's mission and how they contribute):

_____

_____

Focus area 2—Describe a behavior that would improve your leadership skills:

_____

_____

Focus area 3—Describe a behavior that would improve your leadership skills:

_____

_____

You will have the opportunity later in this chapter and in chapters in Part II to update and/or add to your list of leadership focus areas.

10.2 ASSESSING YOUR LEADERSHIP BEHAVIORS

Having defined leadership as a behavior, let's continue the journey to improve your leadership habits. The URL for a leadership-behavior assessment is provided following this paragraph. Complete the five-minute questionnaire by typing or pasting the URL into your web browser:

www.jrosspub.com/CLT

When viewing the scores, keep in mind that they are an indicator and not an absolute evaluation. After completing the questionnaire, click the _Calculate my scores_ button and enter your overall score, as well as the scores for each functional area of the following list:

Overall Score: _____

1. **Score above 90**—Excellent! You have terrific leadership skills!
2. **Score 65 to 89**—You have good leadership skills. You may sometimes have challenges when you are in a leadership role. Review your scores and focus your skill development in areas with lower scores.
3. **Score below 64**—There are significant opportunities for you to improve as a leader. Make note of the areas with the greatest opportunities for improvement and focus on those areas as you journey through this book.

Next, fill out your component scores from the assessment. A score below 15 is an indication of an area where improving your leadership behavior will enhance your leadership skills:

1. Trust: _____

2. Compassion: _____

3. Vision for the future: _____

4. Achieving results: _____

5. Stability/Security: _____

The following is provided to assist you in discovering where opportunities exist for you to improve your leadership behaviors. As you read through the material, keep in mind that you will be asked later in the chapter to confirm or modify your leadership focus areas that were identified earlier.

10.3 WHAT LEADERS SAY

The Gallup organization, in its exhaustive study of people in leadership positions, identified four domains of leadership strengths:[5]

1. **Executing**—means getting things done. Often, the leader will get things done through others, but there is a clear focus on results and providing what people need in order to achieve those results. The ability to execute separates high-performance teams from ordinary teams. Great leaders will flex their style to adapt to circumstances. In one instance they may be more directive, in another more of a coach, and in another they may focus on removing barriers that block the teams' ability to achieve results.

2. **Influencing**—means ensuring that people are committed to moving toward a common goal. People can ignore the leader, comply with a leader's requests (e.g., give the minimum), or they can commit (e.g., give what is required to reach the goal). The challenge is to influence his/her constituents to sign on to the leader's vision of the future and work to achieve it. Finding a compelling answer to "What's in it for my constituents?" is crucial when seeking their commitment.

3. **Relationship-building**—helps people trust their leader. Leaders are committed to balancing the needs of the organization with the needs of the individuals within the organization. Chapter 6 addressed much more about the importance of building relationships.

4. **Strategic thinking**—means the leader keeps people focused on the future that *could be*. Leaders constantly absorb and analyze information and help the team adapt/recover and move forward. They have a compelling view of the future and how the present impacts the journey ahead. With a plan to achieve that view of the future in mind, leaders work at removing what is in the way of progress and provide the resources (including people) that support this goal.

10.4 WHY PEOPLE FOLLOW

Much has been written about leadership from the perspective of specific individuals. For example:

1. Jack Welch, the CEO of General Electric from 1981 to 2001, in his book *Winning*[6]
2. Donald Philips' exposé on political leaders in *The Founding Fathers on Leadership*[7]
3. Peter Drucker's work on role of leaders in *The Effective Executive*[8]

There is good advice about leadership from these sources. However, a person is a leader only if they have followers. Warren Buffett, the legendary investor, pointed out that "a leader is someone who gets things done through other people."

Let's add perspective to the role of leaders by listening to what followers say. What do followers think about their leaders? Why do they follow? What needs do leaders satisfy so that people will follow them? To answer this question, the Gallup organization conducted a formal study involving more than 10,000 followers and found four concepts that consistently arose from the data:[9]

1. **Trust** (also associated with honesty, integrity, and respect)— Webster's dictionary tells us that trust is the "assured reliance on the character, ability, strength, or truth of someone or something."[10] Donald Ferrin and Kurt Dirk's research on trust in leadership asserts that "trust reflects constructs, such as the reliability, integrity, honesty, and fairness of a leader."[11] The research also points out that trusted leaders demonstrate caring and compassion for others.

Patrick Lencioni argues that trust is about demonstrating vulnerability. That is to say, team members who trust one another are not afraid to admit their weaknesses, fears, and failures. Consequently, team members who trust are less likely to engage in hidden agendas or other behaviors that waste everyone's time.[12] Lencioni's concept of vulnerability as a basis of trust must be included with honesty and transparency.

To clarify this point, being honest with oneself and transparent in the sense of sharing information and consequences that may be unpleasant and reflect poorly on the performance of the leader and/or the organization includes the concept of vulnerability.

THE POWER OF TRUST

One of the authors was at the Continental Airlines Maintenance Terminal at George Bush Intercontinental Airport in Houston, Texas, interviewing mechanics about a new maintenance system that was being considered. This was shortly after 9/11. One of the mechanics commented that the CEO, Gordon Bethune, had announced in his weekly call that there would likely be significant furloughs and perhaps some layoffs because of the shutdowns required to prevent future terrorist attacks and the reluctance/fear people had with air travel. In a telling moment about the corporate culture at Continental, another mechanic chimed in, "Yeah, I heard him, and Gordon will get us through this."

In fact, Continental furloughed thousands, as did other airlines, but most were hired back within two years, and Continental maintained its position of leadership in customer satisfaction and on-time departures and arrivals throughout the difficult times. Clearly, people at Continental trusted Gordon Bethune.

In the Continental example, Bethune demonstrated transparency. He did not hide the truth, was up front about likely consequences, and worked hard in order to keep people employed and comply with new safety standards so the airline could resume service.

Besides this anecdotal evidence, there is statistical evidence that trust in leadership is important. Trust in leadership has shown to be positively related to job performance, job satisfaction, organizational commitment, goal commitment, and belief in information—and negatively related to the intention to quit.

10.7   KEY TAKEAWAYS

The key takeaways from this chapter include:

1. Everyone has the opportunity to lead in their work environment and in their personal life.
2. Leadership is a learned behavior.
3. Leadership is not a position; it is the art of getting someone to get something done because they want to do it.
4. Leaders exhibit behaviors that are attributed to leaders or managers depending on circumstances.
5. You have completed the leadership assessment questionnaire and understand the material in this chapter.
6. There is not one universal leadership strength. Leaders can be effective by leveraging many different strengths.
7. People follow leaders whom they trust, who care about them, and who provide stability in the present and hope for the future.
8. You have identified no more than three leadership behavior focus areas. You can update and/or add to your leadership focus areas throughout the remaining chapters in Part II.

ENDNOTES

1. Arruda, William. 2016. "9 Differences Between Being a Leader and a Manager." Retrieved January 1, 2021, from *Forbes Inc.* at https://www.forbes.com/sites/williamarruda/2016/11/15/9 -differences-between-being-a-leader-and-a-manager/#380cce 474609.
2. Murphy, Mark. 2019. *Styles of Leadership—How to Discover and Leverage Yours.* Amazon Press: Books.
3. Llopis, Glenn. 2013. "The Most Successful Leaders Do 15 Things Automatically Every Day." Retrieved January 15, 2021, from *Forbes* at https://www.forbes.com/sites/glennllopis/2013/02/18/ the-most-successful-leaders-do-15-things-automatically-every -day/?sh=5a1be46b69d7.
4. Owen, Jo. 2020. *The Leadership Skills Handbook: 100 Essential Skills You Need to be a Leader. 5th Edition.* London, UK. Kogan Page. October 2020.

5. Rath, Tom and Barry Conchie. 2008. *Strengths Based Leadership: Great Leaders, Teams, and Why People Follow.* New York, NY. Gallup Press. p. 23.

6. Welch, Jack and Suzy Welch. 2005. *Winning.* New York, NY. Harper Business.

7. Phillips, Donald T. 1977. *The Founding Fathers on Leadership.* New York, NY. Warner Books.

8. Drucker, Peter F. 2006. *The Effective Executive: The Definitive Guide to Getting the Right Things Done.* New York, NY. Harper Collins.

9. Rath, Tom and Barry Conchie. 2008. *Strengths Based Leadership: Great Leaders, Teams, and Why People Follow.* New York, NY. Gallup Press. p. 82.

10. *Webster's Ninth Collegiate Dictionary.* 1988. Merriam-Webster. Springfield, MA.

11. Ferrin, Donald L. and Kurt T. Dirks. 2002. "Trust in Leadership: Meta-Analytic Findings and Implications for Research and Practice." *Journal of Applied Psychology* 87, no. 4, pp. 611–628.

12. Lencioni, Patrick. 2005. *Overcoming the Five Dysfunctions of a Team—A Field Guide.* San Francisco, CA. Jossey-Bass. p. 13.

13. Ferrin, Donald L. and Kurt T. Dirks. 2002. "Trust in Leadership: Meta-Analytic Findings and Implications for Research and Practice." *Journal of Applied Psychology* 87, no. 4, pp. 611–628.

14. Rath, Tom and Barry Conchie. 2008. *Strengths Based Leadership: Great Leaders, Teams, and Why People Follow.* New York, NY. Gallup Press. p. 85.

15. Evans, Philip and Thomas S. Wurster. 2000. *Blown to Bits—How the New Economics of Information Transforms Strategy.* Boston, MA. Harvard Business School Press.

16. Hamel, Gary. 2000. *Leading the Revolution.* Boston, MA. Harvard Business School Press.

17. Buckingham, Marcus and Curt Coffman.1999. *First Break All the Rules—What the World's Greatest Managers Do Differently.* New York. Simon & Schuster.

18. Rath, Tom and Barry Conchie. 2008. *Strengths Based Leadership: Great Leaders, Teams, and Why People Follow.* New York, NY. Gallup Press. p. 87.

19. Rath, Tom and Barry Conchie. 2008. *Strengths Based Leadership: Great Leaders, Teams, and Why People Follow.* New York, NY. Gallup Press. p. 89.

20. Tuffley, David. 2020. *Leading Integrated Teams in Virtual Environments—The Definitive Guide to Process-Driven Leadership.* Amazon Press.

21. Dennis, Donna, Deborah Meola, and M. J. Hall. 2013. "Effective Leadership in a Virtual Workforce." Retrieved June 2021 from *TD Magazine* at https://www.td.org/magazines/td-magazine/effective -leadership-in-a-virtual-workforce.

22. "Virtual Collaboration: Rules of the Road. Survey Report October 2020." Retrieved July 18, 2021, from *The American Productivity and Quality Center* at https://www.apqc.org/system/files/ resource-file/2020-11/K011065_Virtual_Collaboration_Rules _Road_Report.pdf.

23. Grzeskowiak, Rachel. 2020. "4 Essential Skills for Virtual Leadership." Retrieved June 8, 2020, from *Biz Library* at https://www .bizlibrary.com/blog/leadership/virtual-leadership-skills/.

24. Conley, Randy. 2020. "12 New Habits for Leading in a Virtual Environment." Retrieved September 22, 2021, from *Ken Blanchard Companies* at https://resources.kenblanchard.com/ blanchard-leaderchat/12-new-habits-for-leading-in-a-virtual -environment.

25. Crenshaw, Dave. 2021. *The Myth of Multitasking: How "Doing it All" Gets Nothing Done. 2nd Edition.* Coral Gables, FL. Mango Publishing.

26. Hanabury, Ethan and Linda Stoddart. 2020. "How to Lead Virtual Teams Successfully." Retrieved June 24, 2021, from *Columbia Business School* at https://www8.gsb.columbia.edu/articles/ columbia-business/how-lead-virtual-teams-successfully.

27. Oldfield, Natalie Doyle. 2020. "Leading in a Virtual Environment: Ten New Guidelines." Retrieved July 12, 2021, from *Forbes* at https://www.forbes.com/sites/forbescoachescouncil/2020/05/ 27/leading-in-a-virtual-environment-ten-new-guidelines/?sh= 5d407c665baf.

CHAPTER 11

TEAM DYNAMICS

"Coming together is a beginning. Keeping together is progress. Working together is success."

—Henry Ford

CHAPTER ROADMAP

A team is greater than a collection of individuals. Great teams are guided to greatness by leaders. Even *self-organizing* teams (a concept made popular by agile project management) benefit from leadership, although the leader may serve more as a coach and servant leader (see Chapter 12 for more on this).

In his 1965 article, "Developmental Sequence in Small Groups," Bruce Tuckman introduced the concept of team development through the stages that he labeled *forming, storming, norming,* and *performing.* He later added a fifth stage, which he called *adjourning* (sometimes called *mourning*). In this chapter we will use Tuckman's stages to explore the leader's role in guiding a team to success. The following list describes the roadmap we will follow:

1. Characteristics of great teams
2. Forming a team
3. Leading through the storm
4. Norming the way
5. Performing for greater results
6. Adjourning
7. Focus area update for team dynamics
8. Reviewing key takeaways from this chapter

11.1   CHARACTERISTICS OF GREAT TEAMS

What are the characteristics of great teams? As a leader, how do you know when your team has developed? The following are some key characteristics of great teams:

1. The team embraces a clearly defined goal or mission and pursues this mission or goal (or set of goals) relentlessly. Team members who do not perform or meet expectations are confronted and dealt with appropriately.
2. Each team member brings a unique skillset and knowledge that contributes to the overall success of the team.
3. Roles and responsibilities are clearly understood by each team member. Boundaries are understood and respected. Levels of authority are established.
4. Team processes are developed. Processes include planning, communications, working, decision making, and conflict resolution. Standards of excellence are established and embraced.
5. Each member commits to delivering results for the team.
6. Team members support each other and recognize each other's accomplishments and contributions.
7. Team members collaborate to establish strong, meaningful relationships.
8. Team members respect each other's competencies and differences.
9. The team becomes resourceful, drawing upon the collective skills to overcome challenges. Great teams are resilient and when they deal with adversity or challenges, they regroup and adapt, if necessary.
10. The leader serves as a catalyst for success.

11.2   FORMING A TEAM

In this initial stage of development, the team requires direction. The leader must be able to articulate the vision for the team. Each team member may bring an understanding—or perhaps a lack of understanding—of the team's mission. An individual team member may resent being *drafted* to the team. The team does not yet have an identity and, therefore, there is confusion among team members. Conflict can exist at different levels.

A team member may question his or her role and the perception of team goals may differ from other team members and the leader.

To successfully move beyond this stage, the leader serves as the chief communicator and director, providing the team's mission. The leader also serves as a catalyst to help team members begin to know each other and start working with each other to understand each other's contributions, knowledge, and skillsets. The challenge for the leader is to blend multiple mindsets into one team mindset. The leader needs to develop individual relationships, establishing the *why* for each team member and defining expectations.

What can you, as a leader, do proactively to effectively manage the forming stage of your team? Here are some thought starters for you to consider:

1. **Have a clearly defined mission**—Whether you are forming a project team, organizing a new team, or inheriting a team, invest time to create a clearly defined mission. What is the *why* for the team? Some guidelines for an effective mission statement include the following:
   - *Make it brief*: Shorter is better than longer. If you can't write it down on the back of a three-by-five-inch index card, it is probably too long.
   - *Make it simple*: Simple can be powerful. Consider Nike's "Just Do It" slogan. The advantage of a simple but powerful mission statement creates an identity and can be easily embraced and repeated by your team members.
   - *Write it down*: Writing your mission statement down may seem obvious, but the process of getting your mission statement written lends itself to refinement. Write it down and create a better mission statement.
   - *Share it*: Communicate the mission statement as often as you can. Communicate it to your team members. Communicate it to your peers and to your interfacing executives.
   - *Make it visible*: Post your mission statement so that all can see it. Let it serve as a constant reminder to your team.
   - *Get buy-in from your team*: The best mission statements are those that are owned by the team. Get your team involved in the process of developing or refining the mission statement.

2. **Know your team**—Meet one-on-one with each team member to understand each member's motives, strengths, personal development needs, and their back story. Refer back to the communications skills that were discussed in Part I of this book. Use the one-on-ones to not only get to know your team members but for the team members to get to know you.

3. **Hold initial briefing sessions**—In the forming stage, it is critical to get that initial buy-in to the team mission through early briefing sessions and to seek alignment from your team members. While the one-on-ones are necessary, it is also critical to open up communications in a team environment and to allow team members to get to know each other.

4. **Set ground rules**—Create ground rules for your team's operating environment. Ground rules (formal or informal) can help establish ways of working together. While the leader may provide some initial ground rules, encourage your team to refine or develop additional ground rules. See Appendix E for an example of team ground rules.

5. **Create a team charter**—A team charter is a document that can establish team values; incorporate the mission statement; record the team's operating environment, constraints, and ground rules; establish guidelines for meetings; and much more. Encourage the team to get involved in the process of developing and maintaining the team charter. Emphasize that it is meant to be a *living* document that is subject to updating when considered necessary by the team.

6. **Create a responsibility assignment matrix (RAM)**—A RAM can be extremely helpful during the forming stage of a team. Simply put, the RAM is a tool that can be used to specifically identify who is responsible for what. A popular form of a RAM is a RACI (responsible, accountable, consult, inform) chart. See the example in Figure 11.1. A RACI chart lists the functions to be performed by the team and then identifies each team member's roles with respect to the functions.

Consider the previously listed thought starters for leading a team through the forming stage. Now consider what else you could do

Functions	Team Lead	John	Jane	Allen	Sue	Rob
- Host weekly meetings	R/A	C	C	C	C	C
- Collect operations data	I	R/A	C	C	C	C
- Produce reports	A		R			
- Conduct daily briefings	A/R	C	C	C	C	C
- Monitor and control costs	A	C	C	R	C	C

Legend:
  R = Responsible; A = Accountable; C = Consult; I = Inform

Figure 11.1   Example of a RACI chart

proactively during this stage. Take a few minutes to list at least two ideas here:

Idea 1 (e.g., lead an icebreaker session to get to know team members in an informal setting. Ask each team member to provide a 2-to-3-minute introduction):

_____

_____

Idea 2:

_____

_____

11.3   LEADING THROUGH THE STORM

Barriers to team success will exist right from the beginning of a team's existence. Each team member brings an individual perspective and may naturally resist the structure of the team environment since it can threaten individuality. Each team member brings his/her ideas of how to work together, differing backgrounds, differing understandings of pace, and problem solving. Conflict occurs as team members express their perspectives and work to overcome differing perspectives and approaches. Additional conflict is introduced when like-minded team members establish cliques, which may differ or detract from the common goal. This tornado of differing views, agendas, personalities, backgrounds, and competition is the *storm* phase of building a team from a group of individuals.

The leader's role throughout the storming stage is to first recognize that the storm exists and then to reconcile the team's differences. The leader should promote each team member's contributions and perspectives while enlisting support for the team's vision and goals.

The upside of the storming stage is that teams can bond when they overcome challenges and adversity. Weathering the storm creates a stronger team identity.

The leader plays a crucial role in guiding the team through these storms and moving the team members toward common goals. Teams can become dysfunctional if they do not move beyond the storming stage.

What can the leader do proactively to effectively manage the storming stage of your team? The following list includes some ideas for you to consider:

1. **Encourage an *open-door* approach**—Promote the idea that your door is always open so team members can vent or share concerns. Team members may be hesitant to raise concerns, but it is important to give them an avenue to share them.

2. **Promote open communications**—Ensure that your team environment allows all team members to voice their ideas, opinions, and perspectives. Team charters and ground rules can help promote this concept. You might consider mini town hall meetings or allowing time in a weekly operational update meeting for open team discussions. Another idea is a weekly *retrospective meeting* where every team member contributes to a conversation about what's working well, what's not working so well, and what can be done better next week.

3. **Consider a *blockers* list**—A blockers list is openly posted and allows all team members to post anything that they believe might be a *blocker* to the progress or productivity of the team. The team should then meet regularly to walk through the list of open blockers. While some of the blockers may need to be resolved by

the team leader, other blockers may require different skillsets or require team buy-in to resolve.

4. **Be quick to recognize conflict**—As the leader, always be aware of your team members' attitudes and be on the lookout for signs of conflict or potential conflict. Do not allow the conflicts to fester (see Section 8.3, *When Should You Resolve Disagreements*). If you recognize cliques forming, address the *why* immediately, or as soon as possible. If a team member appears to check out, find out why. Refer back to Section 4.3 in Chapter 4 (*Sharpening Your Listening Skills*) where we addressed nonverbal communications. Consider the nonverbal signals that may indicate disagreements or issues.

Consider the previously listed ideas for leading a team through the storming stage. Now consider what else you could do proactively during this stage. Take a few minutes to list at least two ideas here:

Idea 1 (e.g., lead the team in a session to establish ground rules for conflict and conflict resolution):

_____

_____

Idea 2:

_____

_____

11.4 NORMING THE WAY

After the storm comes the calm. In the *norming* phase, the members begin to seek harmony and learn to work with each other, respecting the differences and contributions of the other members. Norms of working together as a team are established. The team is no longer a collection of individuals. Team members understand that they are a part of the whole, and a team identity is established. Group processes are established and supported.

The leader plays a pivotal role in guiding the team to develop, establish, and promote team processes. The leader provides members with the authority to make decisions. What can the leader do proactively to effectively manage the norming stage of your team? Here are some strategies for you to consider:

1. **Celebrate successes**—Consider ways to celebrate success, whether it is meeting a certain milestone, achieving a breakthrough, or meeting an operational objective. These can be formal or informal. You should consider allowing the team to define the methods for celebrating successes. Bring the team together to achieve small victories quickly. When the team sees success, they will work together to achieve more successes. Even the *holdouts* will likely join in to become part of the success story.

2. **Encourage team-developed processes**—While a team charter, if you have one, can help establish some initial operating processes, encourage the team to develop their own processes that continue to enhance the welfare and productivity of the team. If you do have a team charter, update the charter with the refined or new processes when they become available. Consider allocating some team time to develop or refine team processes. Even a minimal amount of time can be a worthwhile investment.

3. **Conduct short daily *stand-up* meetings**—This technique (borrowed from the world of agile project management) brings the team together for no more than 15 minutes to allow the team to share progress and concerns. To make these meetings effective, do not use them to solve problems or to have lengthy discussions on any topic. One recommended format is to ask three questions:
   • What did you do yesterday?
   • What will you do today?
   • What is in your way?
   Standing up promotes the idea that the meeting will be short. The team leader is responsible for the effectiveness of the daily meeting, ensuring that the meeting is kept short and that the focus remains on the primary questions.

4. **Consider openly posted progress charts**—Use charts to visibly represent progress for your team. If you are leading a project team, you can use these charts to display progress against project milestones. If your team has an operational focus, use these charts to display results versus predetermined operational metrics.

Consider the above strategies for leading a team through the norming stage. Now consider what else you can do proactively during this stage. Take a few minutes to list at least two ideas here:

Idea 1 (e.g., look for opportunities to creatively post team successes, such as a written headline in a public space or posting on a shared social platform):

Idea 2:

11.5 PERFORMING FOR GREATER RESULTS

When the team reaches the *performing* stage, they are no longer a collection of individuals. They work together in harmony, capitalizing on each other's strengths. Interpersonal relationships are strong. All members work to achieve common goals. Team members support and recognize each other's accomplishments. The team becomes highly effective at solving problems.

Not every team achieves the performing stage. It is up to the leader to guide and orchestrate the team in achieving this level of competence. The leader becomes a coach, not only coaching for overall team performance but for individual performance as well.

Leading a team toward becoming a high-performance team is the primary topic for Chapter 13, *Good Teams to Great Teams*.

11.6 ADJOURNING

Adjourning can occur whenever a team terminates its mission or purpose for any reason. Typically, operational teams are not expected to adjourn unless some sort of reorganization or merger occurs, or the operational team is disbanded for a business reason. Adjourning, though, becomes part of the normal life cycle for project teams.

The process of adjourning can be stressful and sometimes painful. There is often a sense of *loss* on the part of the team members who often feel success through the team effort, as well as on an individual basis. They have developed a sense of comfort with the team environment and now must move on to other opportunities or challenges.

The leader's role during adjourning is to serve as counselor, understanding each team member's motivation and anxiety. This is a great opportunity to communicate one on one and to establish bonds that go beyond the team environment. The leader can add great value by anticipating team members' needs and facilitating or guiding them to the next opportunity or project.

11.7   FOCUS AREA UPDATE FOR TEAM DYNAMICS

Consider the lessons presented in this chapter and the ideas you listed regarding team dynamics and the development of teams. What can you do to enhance your ability as a leader to guide your teams to greater maturity and performance? Take an opportunity to consider your focus areas.

FOCUS AREAS FOR CHAPTER 11

Focus area 1—Describe a behavior that would improve your ability to lead a team through the stages of team development (e.g., when forming a new team, proactively seek to understand each team member's motivations):

_____

_____

Focus area 2—Describe a behavior that would improve your ability to lead a team through the stages of team development:

_____

_____

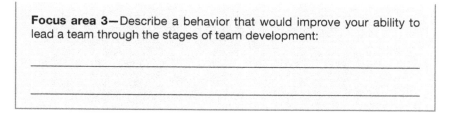

Focus area 3—Describe a behavior that would improve your ability to lead a team through the stages of team development:

_____

_____

Don't forget to update the template you downloaded from www.jross pub.com/CLT to keep track of your focus areas created in exercises throughout this book.

11.8   KEY TAKEAWAYS

The key takeaways from this chapter include:

1. Every team goes through a maturity process. Understand this process to be more effective leading your team as it matures.
2. Bruce Tuckman defines five stages of team development: forming, storming, norming, performing, and adjourning.
3. As a leader, you can be proactive in facilitating a team through these maturity stages.
4. As you adjourn your team, consider the human factors and assist in the process of transitioning members to new opportunities or projects.

CHAPTER **12**

COACHING FOR SUCCESS

"Really, coaching is simplicity. It's getting players to play better than they think that they can."

—Tom Landry

CHAPTER ROADMAP

Great leaders flex their behaviors to adapt to specific circumstances, e.g., sometimes directing, sometimes supporting, sometimes coaching, etc. This chapter will focus on the role of a leader as a coach. As a coach, you develop your team members to achieve successful outcomes. You may often be in the position of coaching your team to a higher level of performance, or to achieve a significant goal or outcome. You will take on the role of coach as you lead your team through the various maturity stages (Tuckman's ladder) that were discussed in Chapter 11. In addition, you may often find yourself coaching an individual member of your team to achieve a higher level of competence, to overcome a performance issue, or perhaps on how to adapt in order to contribute effectively to the team's success. The following list describes the roadmap we will follow:

1. Accountability for results
2. Characteristics of an effective coach
3. The continuous cycle of coaching
4. Coaching the team
5. Focus area update for coaching for success
6. Reviewing key takeaways from this chapter

12.1   ACCOUNTABILITY FOR RESULTS

Leaders are accountable for the results of the team and are responsible for coaching the team and individual team members to achieve desired outcomes. Developing and sharpening your coaching skills will be an investment for the success of the team you are leading. Direct your coaching efforts to the team's vision or desired performance outcomes. Your coaching challenge is to coach individual team members to contribute to overall team success. As the leader, you have *skin in the game* and may have to make hard decisions when an individual team member's performance and development does not align with the team's success. To emphasize this point, consider the two following situations:

- **Situation 1**—Joe is the owner of a small training service company that specializes in technical training. He leads a team of 10 trainers. Success for the team and the organization is defined by customer retention, a high level of repeat business, and bottom-line results. In order to maintain this level of success, each trainer must maintain multiple competencies: training, technical expertise, customer service, student rapport, and marketing. An individual trainer's performance can be measured by student evaluations, customer surveys, assessments of student performance after training, and new sales revenue from the client being served. Joe hires Stacy after attending one of Stacy's seminars. He was impressed with her technical knowledge, but recognized that her training skills required improvement. Joe felt that Stacy was trainable and coachable. After an orientation period, which included train the trainer sessions and partnering on training assignments, Stacy is assigned to lead training for a client. Joe receives negative feedback from the client and works with Stacy to address the feedback. During these coaching sessions, both Stacy and Joe come to the conclusion that, while she has a high level of technical expertise, her people and business skills require development. In addition, Stacy admits that her personal development objectives, which focus on her technical expertise, are not congruent with the training position. Joe decides that it is in the better interest of the team, and company, for Stacy to transition off the team and to pursue a technical opportunity with another company. As the leader, Joe is accountable for the results of the team and may be placed in the position of having to prioritize the team's success over an individual's personal success when the two are not aligned.

- **Situation 2**—Adam is a trainer on Joe's team and consistently performs well. Adam's long-term objective is to start his own training and consulting business, but he knows that he requires more personal development in business development skills. While on Joe's team, Adam recognizes that he can continue to develop with each opportunity, but feels that he needs to accelerate his growth in business development. Adam hires Erin as a personal career coach. As Adam's coach, Erin focuses her coaching effort on Adam's career development and specifically on helping Adam improve his business development skills. Erin holds herself accountable to Adam's success, but not to the success of Joe's team. Assuming successful coaching, Adam may continue to engage Erin as a coach after he transitions to start his own company.

In Situation 1, Joe, as the leader, is accountable for the results of his team and uses his coaching skills to augment his leadership skills. In Situation 2, coaching is Erin's primary skillset, and she focuses her coaching efforts on Adam's development, not Joe's team.

12.2 CHARACTERISTICS OF AN EFFECTIVE COACH

There are times when a leader may coach a team or an individual with the goal of achieving higher levels of performance. In those situations, the leader may find it necessary to migrate from the leader/manager tendencies of simply providing a vision in order to inspire, to directly participating in the development process as a coach. This involves problem solving, providing guidance, and partnering with the team and individual performers to achieve successful outcomes.

Some leaders assume that coaching is directing or just providing specific feedback, but it is much more. Coaching is a different mindset; it is a mindset that focuses on harnessing the intrinsic motivation of the individual performers who make up a team.

What characteristics distinguish an effective coach? See Figure 12.1 for a list. We will explore these in more detail in this section.

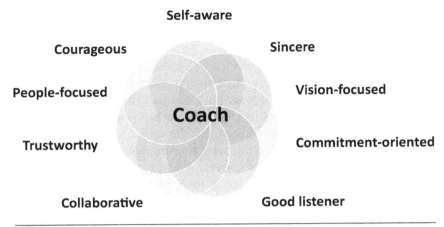

Figure 12.1   Characteristics of an effective coach

1. **Self-aware**—An effective coach understands how his or her beliefs, feelings, and limitations can be leveraged as strengths, while partnering with others to compensate for any weaknesses. By being self-aware, a coach is in a better position to *let go* when it is important to let go and is more open to different and creative ways to interact with team members. In addition, it is important that a coach does not allow their emotions and characteristics to influence their interactions.

2. **Sincere**—An effective coach will sincerely seek improvement in the person being coached. The *reward* is the growth.

3. **Vision-focused**—An effective coach knows how to set a vision, communicate it clearly and in detail, and maintain a focus on that vision. A successful coach can *see* the potential future in spite of criticism or skepticism.

4. **Commitment-oriented**—Having set expectations, the effective coach is also skilled at obtaining commitments from the team and the individual performers. The coach ensures alignment on expected outcomes and the changes needed to achieve those outcomes.

5. **Good listener**—An effective coach is an effective listener who embraces the listening skillset that we addressed earlier in this book. Active listening is key to promoting collaboration and continuous improvement. The effective coach should listen to seek understanding.

6. **Collaborative**—Instead of directing the team or individual performers to achieve outcomes, the effective coach embraces collaborative approaches. The leader, as a coach, does not have all the answers. The best ideas and approaches come from the team, either through individual contributions or through collaborative discussions. The coach should serve as the linchpin for these collaborative discussions by encouraging an open and safe environment to raise ideas and views in order to achieve alignment on goals.

7. **Trustworthy**—The effective coach develops a personal connection with those they coach. Through that connection the coach builds an environment of trust. The team as a whole and individual performers on the team must trust the coach on multiple levels, such as with confidentiality, sincerity, well-being, knowledge, risk-taking, and doing the right thing, to name a few.

8. **People-focused**—Effective coaches are people-focused. They work to understand each individual performer's motives, perspectives, feelings, strengths, and weaknesses. They work at understanding the *why* for each team member and work at achieving harmony with multiple *whys*, along with the team goals and aspirations.

9. **Courageous**—The effective coach is courageous in providing feedback and in being honest in all interactions (see Chapter 5 for more information on receiving and giving feedback). The effective coach is courageous by being willing to take risks. The coach is willing to ask the tough questions and to directly address the elephant in the room. Lack of courage may lead to the coach holding back because of fear of endangering their relationships or how they are perceived by team members. The effective coach understands that while most people may prefer kind feedback, accurate feedback is more important.

From the previous list, identify what you believe to be the three most impactful characteristics of an effective coach:

1. _____

2. _____

3. _____

12.3   THE CONTINUOUS CYCLE OF COACHING

"The biggest room in the world is the room for improvement."

—Helmut Schmidt

Coaching is a continuous process that only ends when the team adjourns or, if you are leading a project, when the project ends. In this section we will explore the continuous cycle of coaching (see Figure 12.2). We will now address the components of this process:

1. **Internalization**—The coaching process begins with the coach. The coach needs to internalize the need, improvement, goal, or outcome of the coaching process. If the focus is a team outcome or objective, then the coach needs to own the vision as articulated in his or her role as a leader. The coaching process will be weakened or fail if the coach cannot articulate the vision and

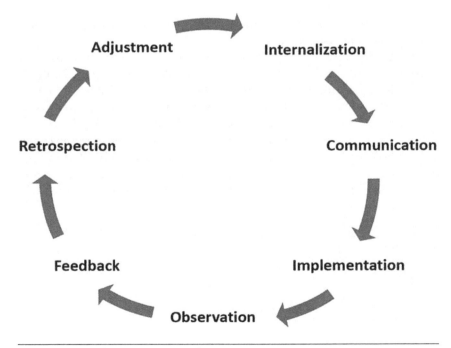

Figure 12.2   The coaching cycle

achieve personal clarity. Details matter. Owning the vision communicates sincerity and commitment. If the focus of the coaching effort is a performance objective or an issue with an individual team performer, the same approach applies. Although the *big picture* is important, the details matter and trump generalities.

2. **Communication**—Although the coach may take the lead in communicating the need, improvement, goal, or outcome, it is important to stress that communication in coaching is not a one-way or top-down process. The coach should encourage open discussion in order to achieve a common understanding. The *how to* for achieving that outcome should be a participative process. The coach should encourage the individual performer or team members to share their thoughts and ideas for implementation. He/She should refrain from directing the approach, but may serve as a sounding board or provide expertise on a peer basis. The coach should also seek emotional and intellectual feedback and commitment from the performer or team members, asking questions such as:

   - What do you think?
   - How do you feel about this approach?
   - How will we know that it was done?
   - How can we measure results? (Is there an opportunity to clarify with metrics?)
   - What's your confidence level?
   - Is it doable?
   - Can you commit to this?

   If you sense some insecurity or a false sense of confidence in team members, a great question to ask is, "What can I do to make you feel more confident?" or alternatively, "What can you or I do to get you to a higher level of confidence?" This may open up more discussion or reveal an opportunity for you or the team member(s) to explore. One of the key goals for this communication is to have the team or team member take ownership and accountability for the actions required.

3. **Implementation**—Implementation of the actions resulting from the communication is left up to the team or the individual performer. The coach should refrain from *directing* or interfering in the implementation process. Letting go is not easy for many leaders but, as a coach, you must let go unless you have a specific

role in the implementation. This process should allow for some adaptation, if needed.

4. **Observation**—During this process, which overlaps implementation, the coach actively observes the action or actions being implemented. The coach collects these observations for assessment and feedback. While the level of investment in the observation step may vary depending on the leader and his or her leadership style (e.g., servant, transformational, problem solving, etc.), the observations may include the following:

   - What worked well?
   - How were results achieved?
   - Were any innovative approaches used?
   - Was adaptation required, and if so, how was this received?
   - What did not work well? Why not?
   - Were there unexpected obstacles?
   - Were there unintended negative results or impacts?
   - If the intended action failed, what were the consequences?
   - What could have been done differently or what behavior can be changed?
   - What were the lessons learned?
   - What were the reactions or impacts from other team members or other participants in the process?

5. **Feedback**—Feedback is essential to the coaching process. The coach should establish a nonthreatening environment to provide frank and courageous feedback to the team or to the individual performer. Trust and credibility are crucial to feedback conversations. As the coach, your role is to provide feedback constructively and in a positive manner. Every feedback conversation is an opportunity to nurture growth while enhancing the relationship. The tone of feedback conversations should be positive and healthy. Try modeling the feedback using the following model, nicknamed the *SMARTC* model (not to be confused with SMART feedback from Chapter 5):

   - **Specific:** Using your observations, be as specific as you can when providing feedback. Use particular examples from your observations and be specific with your recommendations. Avoid general or vague statements. When providing recommendations, support your recommendations with reasons and benefits.

- **Motivational:** Your feedback should be motivational and positive. It should encourage the team or individual to embrace your feedback and take action. When providing praise, it is important to be sincere and authentic. Even criticism can be presented in a motivational manner. Remember that your role is to enhance the development of the team or individual performer. You and your feedback are serving the best interests of the team and the individual performer.
- **Analytical:** Be analytical without being judgmental. Refer back to the facts and your observations. Use your perspective, experience, and insights to share what worked and what didn't work, along with what can be improved. Be open to dialogue and receiving feedback on your feedback.
- **Responsive:** Be responsive to the needs of the team or the individual performer. When providing feedback to an individual performer, tailor your feedback to him or her, taking into account his or her experience level, motives, attitudes, and perspectives.
- **Thoughtful:** Be thoughtful and sensitive of the emotional state of the performer, remembering that everyone is different. Choose your words carefully to ensure that you do not unintentionally offend or insult the performer. Focus on the performance, not the performer.
- **Conclusive:** Your feedback conversations should lead to solid conclusions or takeaways. Do not leave the conversation hanging. Always agree on the next action. Be open to other models as well and be willing to experiment to find the model that works best for your team and your situation.

6. **Retrospection**—As identified through feedback, initiate *look-back* and/or performance review sessions to evaluate the specific actions that may need to be implemented. In addition, take time to discuss the coaching process. Was it beneficial? What worked? What could be improved? What can we do differently?

7. **Adjustment**—Following retrospection, commit and obtain commitment to adjust behaviors and/or to implement actions defined in the retrospection. New actions may initiate new coaching opportunities.

12.4 COACHING THE TEAM

Coaching the entire team to achieve a goal or improve performance introduces challenges to the coach. Some of these challenges are listed here:

1. Each team member brings different levels of experience, perspectives, and attitudes.
2. Each team member is at a different stage of personal development.
3. Each team member is motivated differently.
4. Communication styles and preferences differ among team members.
5. Backgrounds, cultures, and personal biases are obstacles in creating team cohesion.
6. Stronger team members may feel hindered by other team members.
7. Weaker team members may feel intimidated by the star players or by the entire team.
8. Personalities may clash, introducing conflict at multiple levels.
9. Work styles differ among the team members.

Coaching the team begins with the *why* for coaching. Why are you trying to achieve this specific result or outcome? Once you are clear on your *why*, implement the coaching cycle—work to overcome obstacles and to orchestrate disparate motives to achieve team goals.

The following list describes some techniques and strategies that will enhance the coaching cycle:

1. **Communicate the vision**—Be persistent about communicating the vision. Use every team interaction to discuss the vision or goal. Keep the vision visible to all team members. Work on obtaining the buy-in to the vision from all team members. During a visit to the NASA space center in 1962, President Kennedy noticed a janitor sweeping the floor. He stopped his tour to approach the janitor and said, "Hi, I'm Jack Kennedy. What are you doing?" The janitor responded, "Well, Mr. President, I'm helping put a man on the moon." That janitor understood the vision and his role in the realization of the vision.
2. **Break the vision into achievable and realistic milestones**—Breaking the vision or goals into smaller chunks facilitates

progress and allows the coach to use those interim milestones for learning and coaching opportunities.

3. **Make progress visible**—Use the team space to post progress reports or to mark milestones that have been reached. Visual charts work best, but keep them easy to understand. It doesn't take much effort, but it does make progress visible.

4. **Enlist every team member individually**—Conduct individual conversations to enlist every team member in the vision. Make it clear to each member that he or she brings value to the team through their individual skills and strengths.

5. **Hold retrospective sessions frequently**—Use frequent retrospective sessions to discuss what has worked well toward achieving the goal or vision and what could be improved. Encourage your team members to promote ideas for improvement and gain buy-in from the team to implement those ideas where feasible.

6. **Encourage team learning**—Build an environment that encourages team learning by providing opportunities for team members to share lessons learned. Encourage formal and informal exchange of ideas.

7. **Enlist the star players to serve as mentors**—By enlisting your star members as mentors, they can contribute to the overall goal or vision by giving back and providing guidance to newer or less-skilled team members.

8. **Embrace the learning cycle**—When the team is required to learn new methods or techniques to achieve a goal, embrace the learning cycle of your team by adapting to the learning stage. A simplified training cycle consists of *training, adapting,* and *mastering.* While in the training cycle, the coach serves as a trainer, providing specific training on new methods, procedures, or techniques. Once the team advances from training, they begin to adapt and incorporate the lessons from the training. In this stage your role as a coach is to ensure that the team members continue to embrace new ways of thinking and executing. This is often done through one-on-one coaching. In the mastering stage, team members have fully adapted to the new ways and are beginning to master new skills and behaviors. The coach now becomes an advisor to the whole team, but team members may have to coach each other on specific performance challenges.

9. **Promote open communication**—Build an environment of trust and open communication. Make the environment safe for members to voice concerns and promote ideas. As a leader and coach, support transparent communication, even when the news may not be positive.

Coaching the team and orchestrating success is a continuous effort and requires dedication, patience, focus, and discipline on the part of the coach. Believe in your team and connect with your team members on a personal level.

12.6   FOCUS AREA UPDATE FOR COACHING FOR SUCCESS

Based on the lessons in this chapter, list your focus areas for improvement.

FOCUS AREAS FOR CHAPTER 12

Focus area 1—Begin embracing the continuous coaching cycle for your team or an individual performer. Describe a behavior that can enhance your coaching skills (e.g., I can improve my coaching skills by providing honest but helpful feedback):

_____

_____

_____

Focus area 2—Begin embracing the continuous coaching cycle for your team or an individual performer. Describe a behavior that can enhance your coaching skills (e.g., hold weekly retrospective meetings with my team to obtain feedback on communications and performance):

_____

_____

_____

Don't forget to update the template you downloaded from www.jross pub.com/CLT to keep track of your focus areas created in exercises throughout this book.

12.7   KEY TAKEAWAYS

The key takeaways from this chapter include:

1. An effective coach is skilled at human interactions and possesses many characteristics that distinguish him or her from other managers and leaders.
2. Coaching is a continuous cycle, comprised of internalization, communication, implementation, observation, feedback, retrospection, and adjustment.
3. Coaching teams to achieve a goal or vision requires orchestration of disparate talents and motives, and presents unique challenges to the coach.
4. Coaching self-organizing teams requires a focus on process.

CHAPTER 13

GOOD TEAMS TO GREAT TEAMS

"Great things in business are never done by one person. They're done be a team of people."

—Steve Jobs

CHAPTER ROADMAP

Very few people are *individual* contributors when engaged in achieving the mission of an organization (organization in the broadest sense of the word—including family, community, neighborhood, workplace, sports teams, etc.). Rather, people are most often involved with others on a team (e.g., the customer service team, the sales team, a project team, or the architectural review committee within the neighborhood association, to name a few). Because people are often engaged in the work of a team, they have the potential and opportunity to be a leader. The question becomes: how can a leader influence the performance of a team in a positive way? The answer to that question is the focus of this chapter. The following list describes the roadmap we will follow:

1. The role of the leader in developing a high-performing team
2. The steps to achieve a high-performing team
   - Trust
   - Commitment to mission
   - Unbridled communication
   - Adapting to change
   - Accountability for results
3. Leadership in self-organizing teams
4. Focus areas for developing high-performing teams
5. Prioritizing leadership focus areas
6. Key takeaways

13.1 DEVELOPING A HIGH-PERFORMING TEAM: THE ROLE OF THE LEADER

In this chapter we present a pathway to achieving the status of a high-performing team in terms of achieving *results* related to the *mission* of the organization, not only today but into the future as well. The pathway to achieving the status of a high-performing team is represented in Figure 13.1.

The five steps on the pathway to a high-performing team are supported/enabled by topics that were previously discussed throughout Parts I and II. While these enablers will not be discussed further in this

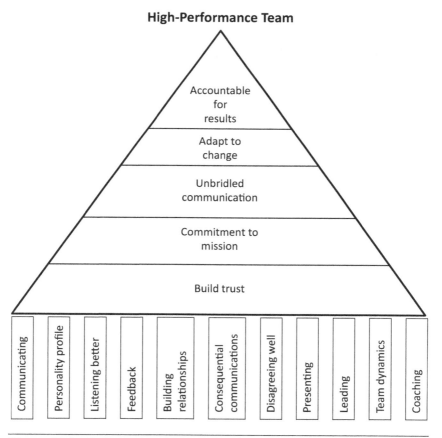

Figure 13.1   Pathway to a high-performing team

chapter, do revisit them when prioritizing your focus areas for improvement at the end of this chapter. For now, let's explore each step in the pathway to creating a high-performing team.

13.2   BUILDING TRUST

In Chapter 10 we established that *trust* is a characteristic of great leaders. You may have identified *building trust* as a focus area in that chapter. In this chapter *building trust* is presented as the foundation on the pathway to a high-performing team. Coming up next, you'll find a brief exercise to help you clarify whether building trust is a priority focus area for you.

Think about the people you trust and what they did that led you to trust them. Take time to list what they did in the space on the next page. Before you complete the exercise, consider this thought-starter list to help you identify specific behaviors:

1. Those who established a personal connection with you, creating a positive relationship (see Chapter 6, *Every Relationship Has Value*)
2. Those who trusted you to deliver on your commitments; who didn't micromanage but were there if you needed help
3. Those who acknowledged and respected everyone's contribution
4. Those who practiced transparency and honesty—who let everyone know what they were thinking and didn't hide the truth or leave you wondering about issues
5. Those who met their commitments, who did what they said they were going to do
6. Those who made decisions that were consistent with the mission of the organization
7. Those who allowed people to question them and their motives without becoming defensive
8. Those who demonstrated competence as a leader and were not afraid to admit when they didn't know something or when they were wrong
9. Those who listened without the intent to respond, but listened to hear (see Chapter 4, *Listen Better to Succeed*)
10. Those who asked for feedback and used it to improve themselves (see Chapter 5, *Receiving and Giving Feedback—Are You Ready?*)

Now, list three to five things the leaders did (their behaviors) that led you to trust her/him (e.g., the leader respected me and was open to listening to my suggestions):

1. _____

2. _____

3. _____

4. _____

5. _____

Are there any behaviors that stand out from the preceding analyses? Are there any behaviors you should do more of, less of, start doing, or stop doing to become a better leader? Consider referencing this list as you choose your *final* leadership focus areas later in the chapter.

13.3   COMMITMENT TO MISSION

In this section we will emphasize commitment to the *mission of the organization*. While teams, departments, business units, etc., can have a mission, it is a paramount responsibility of leaders to assure the alignment of all parts of the organization with its overall mission. That is to say, to assure that the members of the organization understand how they contribute value to the purpose of the organization. When the purpose of the organization is top of mind with its members, the results can be powerful.

THE RITZ CARLTON COMMITMENT TO MISSION

Cesar Ritz, who founded the Ritz Hotels (later to be included in the Ritz Carlton Hotel Group), injected his organization with the mission of customer service with the phrase, "The customer is always right." Each person at the Ritz Carlton, at all levels, is empowered to spend up to $2,000 per guest per incident (not per year) to assure customer issues are quickly addressed. The amount matters less than the trust that Ritz

Carlton shows to its employees to achieve the mission. Today, the company operates 108 hotels in 30 countries and is regularly at the top of the Zagat list for its hotel and dining services. It has also won the Malcolm Baldrige National Quality Award twice! It is the only member of the hospitality industry to do so.

With commitment to mission, the need for rules, oversight, and management control, while still necessary, is significantly reduced. The following list contains suggestions as to how leaders can build commitment to the mission of the organization:

1. *What* an organization measures is vitally important in promoting and underpinning a commitment to its mission. Consequently, measuring and reporting on the impact of employee commitment is one way to nurture that commitment, such as:
   - Provide efficient ways for customers/vendors/other stakeholders to provide feedback about employees who have provided excellent service or other components of the mission and publicize those stories throughout the organization. It is necessary to mine feedback for opportunities to improve and commit resources toward achieving those improvements.
   - Support employees who work to uphold company values regarding topics that may include climate change, diversity, helping the homeless, etc., and then publicize the efforts and results.
   - Reduce the company's mission to metrics (not typical financial measures). Examples include customer response time, number of employee accidents (both on and off the job), carbon emission, community support activities, and employee turnover. Track those metrics and publicize the progress. Ask employees to help define the metrics.
2. In his groundbreaking work about motivation in the workplace, Fredrick Hertzberg discovered factors that when present led to job satisfaction (called *motivators*) and other factors when absent led to job dissatisfaction (called *hygiene*).[1] To increase commitment, maximize the impact of motivators and minimize hygiene:
   - Satisfiers (motivators):
     - Challenging work
     - Opportunities for advancement

- □ A path to more responsibility
- □ Opportunities to achieve
- □ Opportunities of personal growth
- Dissatisfiers (hygiene):
  - □ Unsatisfactory working conditions; in the post-pandemic world, this may include not providing equipment to work virtually or not allowing people to work remotely
  - □ A lack of competitive pay and benefits
  - □ Not addressing the needs of specific groups of workers, such as childcare needs, needs of handicapped workers, etc.
  - □ Overbearing/nonvalue-adding policies and rules
3. Apply the DCOM Model:
   - D—Clear *direction* about what is expected in work output and that it contributes to achieving the mission of the organization. Explain the expectations. What do expected results look like? Confirm that people understand the expectation (e.g., use active listening skills).
   - C—People have the *competencies* needed to achieve the expected results. There may be a need for training, job shadowing, internships, job rotation, and opportunities for continuing education. Ensure team members have the skills, both technical and soft, to complete assigned tasks. If not, support with training, mentoring, or coaching.
   - O—People have the *opportunity* to meet expectations. Ensure that they have enough time to get the job done. Confirm that people have the time required to achieve expected results (e.g., people are not overcommitted). Have team members report to each other their progress on commitments. Provide support and guidance where it is needed. Confirm that team members are comfortable with reporting when they have problems or encounter barriers preventing the achievement of commitments.
   - M—Help maintain the *motivation* of employees by providing meaningful work and metrics that show progress/movement toward objectives. Confirm that team members want to complete tasks, that they understand how their work product advances the team's progress, the consequences of not meeting expectations, and the impact on the organization and coworkers if they do not meet expectations.

4. Implement clear strategies for employee engagement. Seek feedback and act on that feedback. These are not suggestion boxes but rather conversations about what is working and not working that lead to actions.

5. Limit organizational hierarchy. While organizational hierarchies are necessary, they so often create roadblocks to fast and effective communication because of the need to obtain permission to act. Many organizations have a habit of creating rules and standards designed to minimize errors rather than maximize success.[2]

6. Eliminate jobs and work that does not have a clear line of sight to the organization's mission. When it is difficult for employees to see and understand how their work matters, it *may* mean that it doesn't. Eliminating nonvalue-adding work usually means eliminating jobs, which can be unpleasant. However, jobs can be repurposed, and people can be transferred to higher value-added work. In instances where there are no opportunities for future employment, those who leave the organization should be treated with respect and fairly in the sense of support from the organization while they seek meaningful work.

13.4 UNBRIDLED COMMUNICATION

When we use the phrase *unbridled communication*, it is not uncommon for people to ask: "Why?" We often hear, "I am drowning in information, emails, texts, Instagrams, and news reports." In order to explain this, it is necessary to take a short ride through the history of organizational practices, starting in the late 1800s with Frederick Taylor's work to improve the efficiency of manufacturing processes.[3] At the 1900 Paris Exposition Universelle, the exhibition of his steel-cutting process was described as miraculous. His process cut 50 ft/min compared to the 9 ft/min that was typical at that time. Taylor did not accomplish the spectacular increase in productivity with new and improved equipment, but rather he reduced the steel-cutting process to discreet steps and optimized each step to improve the output of the process; for example, temperature of the incoming steel, distance between the worker and the machine, distance between the worker and the steel, how the steel was fed into the cutting machine, etc. The steelworker no longer produced a piece of finished cut steel; rather, he completed specific steps:

1. Pull a piece of steel from the rack
2. Assure temperature is between X and Y degrees Fahrenheit
3. Place steel on the input table
4. Adjust the angle to 15 degrees from the horizontal
5. Lock steel jaws onto steel plate
6. Turn feed motor on

The steelworker did not need to make decisions and, therefore, did not need information. The steelworker just followed steps, and the result was predictable. We have become addicted to Taylor's improved efficiency over the last 100 years.

Fast-forward to the early twenty-first century where the number of interactions within and among systems have become much more dense, such that small disturbances can have a monumental impact. We have moved from a world that is complicated to a world that is far more complex.

COMPLICATED VERSUS COMPLEX

Complicated systems may have many moving parts, but the behavior of the parts is dictated by rules, such that an adjustment to one part has a defined impact on other parts. That is to say, outcomes can be *predicted*.

The gasoline engine in an automobile is complicated, with many moving parts. But the behavior of the engine is predictable. It follows specific laws of physics and chemistry—press on the accelerator and the car goes faster. Taylor's solutions evolved in complicated systems and the impact of his work is still evident today.

On the other hand, complex systems are characterized by a dense interaction of variables within the system and interactions of variables outside the system, such that outcomes caused by a defined input are difficult, if not impossible, to predict. Complex systems tend to evolve in response to the density of interactions and the speed in which those interactions occur. Many of the interactions and their impact on the system may be unknown; a solution that works at one point in time will fail at another point in time.

Taylor's legacy has led many leaders and managers to apply solutions designed for a complicated problem to a problem with high complexity. Consider the COVID-19 pandemic that spread around the world beginning in late 2019, and that is still with us in 2022—the world responded as though a desired set of actions would give predictable results.[4]

When organizations continue to apply solutions that were designed for complicated situations to complex situations, the solutions may be inadequate and disastrous in the extreme.

To adapt to the complexity that exists in the world today, decision making is pushed down in the organization. There will not be time for complicated processes where rules, procedures, and standards are reviewed in order to make decisions where outcomes are predictable. In a world of increasing complexity, organizations will decentralize decision making where people at lower levels in the organization have more relevant and timely information in their area of expertise than those at higher levels. To provide more context about the entire system of the organization, these empowered decision makers will need more information about the entire system and how components interact to impact outcomes. Communication of this information at all levels of the organization must increase for organizations to manage complexity. However, unbridling communication to release information into the hands of the decentralized decision makers may not be consistent with the norms of the organization for a number of reasons, including:

1. People don't have time to share information.
2. "It's not my job." People don't get recognized or rewarded for sharing information.
3. It is not relevant to their job. People should just do their job and leave the decisions to managers/leaders.
4. Information is power and not to be shared.
5. People lower in the organization don't have a need to know.
6. There are no systems in place to share information efficiently and effectively.
7. Also, what information, to whom, and when?

COMPLEXITY AT THE SUEZ CANAL

Container ships, introduced in the 1980s, could hold between 4,000 and 5,000 TEUs (twenty-foot equivalent units). The size of container ships since the 1980s have increased dramatically, where today the ultra-high-capacity container ships can carry up to 22,000 TEUs with designs for vessels up to 27,000 TEUs in the works. In response to the increasing size of container ships, the Suez Canal was expanded in 2014 at a cost of US$9 billion. The Panama Canal completed an expansion in 2016 at a cost in excess of US$6 billion. The input was bigger ships; the output was wider and deeper canals. Problem solved.

On March 23, 2021, the ultra-high-capacity container ship, Ever Given, with a capacity of 20,000 TEUs (it was carrying 18,000 TEUs at the time

(continues)

of the accident) was hit by a crosswind, and the 400-meter-long container ship lodged into the 205-meter-wide Suez Canal. The ship was finally set free on March 29. By the time it was able to move, over 400 ships were queued on either end of the canal, holding up to 3.3 million tons of trade per hour, valued at $400 million. Egyptian authorities demanded almost $1 billion in damages from the owners of the Ever Given, and there are untold lawsuits lining up from other carriers.

Authorities are now suggesting that human error and technology may have contributed to the accident. This statement highlights the complexity of moving large container ships around the world. Not only is the movement through the canals complex, but these larger ships impact the systems at ports, loading and unloading cranes, and support vessels that are rushing to catch up. However, the solutions may not be relevant in the three to five years it takes to catch up. The cargo industry may well have changed by then.

The key questions then become: what information needs to be communicated, to whom, when, and how? The recommendations for leaders to take into account in order to answer the questions include:

1. Empower teams that are making decisions to decide what information they need, how often, and in what form. The purpose of the increased communication is to provide more context for the decisions and to increase the line of sight to the mission of the organization, and consequently, to make better decisions. Encourage teams to experiment and learn. Let them share experiences with other teams.

2. Colocate teams, if not physically, then virtually. Having team members colocate has been shown to increase communication and engagement.[5]

3. Rotate people through different departments. For example, engineers through finance, finance through manufacturing, manufacturing to accounting, etc.

4. Stanley McChrystal in his book *Team of Teams*[6] formed a team of teams. One member from each team joins another team. Members of the team of teams share information and bring that back to their original teams:
   - What is working and not working
   - Opportunities for improvement

- Connections/interdependencies among teams
- How to increase success of the mission
- Which *experiments* worked and which ones didn't

5. In meetings at the team, department, or organizational level, spend time talking about the interconnectedness that exists within the system, the need for trust, and the need for more communication, in order to develop a culture that supports the sharing of communication.

6. Establish a practice where teams, departments, business units, etc., set up ground rules for managing the pandemic of instant communication that includes emails, text messages, and the myriad of social media applications. Much of it is causing more distractions than producing value for people. Have teams discuss and make recommendations to manage these distractions.

13.5 ADAPT TO CHANGE

It was pointed out earlier that many management and leadership practices in use today were in part developed under Frederick Taylor's reductionist philosophy. Reductionist in the sense of reducing complicated processes to underlying steps and then optimizing each step to achieve outcomes with less energy, time, and change. As the number of interactions and interdependencies within a system increase, it is difficult, if not impossible, to predict outcomes. Rather, as complexity increases it is necessary for organizations to adapt quickly to change to become more flexible in dealing with challenges. When complexity is low, results are more predictable and the organization can rely more on rules, procedures, and standards. As complexity increases, the organization must adapt to change, become more agile and flexible, and be willing to experiment and recover.

To clarify, we are not saying this is no place for rules, procedures, and standards in complex situations. We are saying that the more complex the environment, the more it will be necessary to delegate decision making down in the organization where people can adapt to circumstances to achieve desired outcomes.

The following true story demonstrates the point.

ADAPTING TO CHANGE

Jonathan was traveling from San Francisco to Houston to catch an international flight to attend an important meeting. His flight arrived many hours before his connecting flight, and he is on a tight schedule when he gets to his final destination. When Jonathan checks in, he is told seats have opened up on an earlier flight. Jonathan would love to get on that earlier flight and alleviate some pressure on his schedule, but he knows his bags are still tagged for the later flight. He will need those bags for a change of clothes and other materials for the meeting. Jonathan is concerned that making the earlier flight is pointless if his bags will be arriving later.

Another agent hears Jonathan's comments and offers to try to get Jonathan's bags off the earlier flight. It is raining outside, so the attendant grabs an umbrella, goes down the jet bridge, down the stairs to the baggage cart, asks a baggage handler to find the bags, and brings them to Jonathan to gate check on the earlier flight.

The following day, Jonathan is recounting the excellent customer service he received when a safety manager attending the meeting approaches Jonathan criticizing the gate agent, stating the agent took unnecessary risks, that he could have slipped on the tarmac, hurt himself, and/or dropped the bags in the rain. Not a good outcome. The safety manager also chastised Jonathan for encouraging the agent to get his bags.

Was the gate agent in error by taking unnecessary risks or was he fulfilling the mission of excellent customer service with acceptable risks? Was Jonathan at fault for not discouraging the agent from retrieving his bags?

Here is some additional information. The airline industry has gone through considerable changes because of incidents in air travel—some catastrophic and others far less so. The industry instituted human factor training for airline crews, mechanics, and eventually down to all levels. Employees are empowered to provide exceptional customer service as long as it does not endanger the safety of the aircraft, the safety of passengers, or their own safety. People at all levels receive training.

The vice president of operations of an airline commented to one of the authors that the leadership of the organization trusts their workers to assess situations, and if safety is not jeopardized and costs are acceptable, they can make a decision and take action. No need to escalate decisions.

In the situation above, the safety manager at the meeting focused on following procedures and rules, regardless of other factors. It may be that, in part, the safety manager had once witnessed or experienced a work-related injury, and his comments came from not wanting to see something like that happen again. We call this the *not on my watch syndrome*. This syndrome causes managers and leaders to implement more rules and procedures so accidents do not occur. While no one can know what the safety manager's motivations were to make the comment to Jonathan, consider the following points:

1. The safety manager was not aware of the airline's human factor training.
2. The safety manager did not trust the attendant to assess the situation appropriately and preferred the default solution—to not take risks without prior approval, follow the process, and seek guidance.
3. The attendant did not go into the aircraft or to the baggage cart but asked a baggage handler, who was already working in the rain, to retrieve the bags (we cannot assume to know what the attendant would have done if the handler could not find the bags).
4. The safety manager considered his mission of safety (which is important) to have priority over other dimensions of the mission, such as providing excellent customer service. Safety trumped all other considerations.

When empowering employees to act, an important consideration is: how much empowerment does an organization allow? At what point does an organization stop delegating decision-making authority? To answer this question, consider the concept of *scope of consequences*. Let's take the airline industry to explain this concept.

Imagine a mechanic is checking the landing gear on an aircraft between flights. Problems with the landing gear can be catastrophic. There are standards and procedures the mechanic must follow to assure that the landing gear is operational. If the mechanic encounters something unusual in his or her work, the mechanic escalates the situation and does not make a decision to bypass standards and procedures. The consequences of a mistake are too severe. Consequently, the aircraft may not be cleared to fly causing flight delays or cancellations and inconvenienced customers.

In the situation where the gate attendant went down to retrieve Jonathan's luggage, the consequences are less severe and the gate agent had been trained to assess the situation before taking action. In many cases, it is not advisable to follow a procedure designed for one set of circumstances and apply it to all other situations.

13.6 ACCOUNTABILITY FOR RESULTS

The pinnacle on the pathway to a high-performing team is being *accountable for results*. Accountability and results are both vitally important. Consequently, they are addressed here as two subjects:

1. **Accountability**—Let's define *accountability* in the context of this chapter because accountability and responsibility are often used interchangeably, but they are not the same thing.

   *The **accountable** person is the individual who is ultimately answerable for the activity or decision. This includes "yes" or "no" authority and veto power. Only one **accountable** person can be assigned to an action. The **responsible** person is the individual(s) who actually completes the task.*[7]

   Responsibility can be shared but only one person is accountable.[8] In this chapter we are discussing a culture of accountability[8] in which:

   - People at all levels take ownership for the strategic results of the organization.
   - Project or work handoffs are complete and progress does not slip through the cracks.
   - People consider how their work contributes to the mission and make adjustments as necessary to align efforts with the mission.
   - People break down barriers and collaborate to achieve the correct results.

   To be clear, the *responsibility* for a task can be *assigned*; however, *accountability* is *accepted*. That is to say, a constituent gets to vote on their level of accountability.

   We often hear stories about holding someone accountable (e.g., leaders hold people accountable for results). However, unless you are willing to hold yourself accountable, it is difficult to hold someone else accountable.

   Consider the interaction of Bill and Eddie in the company's coffee bar after a meeting:

2. Teamwork: Team members work as a team rather than as a group of individuals as they move through the steps in the Tuckman ladder.
3. Trust: See Section 13.2.
4. Commitment: See Section 13.3.
5. Continuity: See Section 10.4.
6. Improvement: the team should continuously improve team member skills and team processes.

Roles for leaders in regarding self-organizing teams:[16]

1. Assemble the team: Because the team will decide how work will get done, it is essential that the "right" people are on the team with the skills needed to be successful (e.g., a cross-functional team). Team members will manage their issues and challenges without management intervention. Consequently, team members must be able to disagree well (see Chapter 8: Disagreeing Well).
2. Clarify roles and constraints: Management declares the results to be expected and sets the boundaries for team activities.
3. Facilitate: There is more facilitation (as opposed to directing) needed to support self-organizing teams. For example, on agile project management teams, the leader may facilitate stand-up meetings, process improvement meetings, and lessons learned to improve processes (see Appendix F for a Facilitation Guide).
4. Remove obstacles and barriers to success. This often involves managing the burden of administrative functions so the team can focus on higher value-added activities and limiting the influence of factors that do not add value to the team's efforts.

13.8 CONCLUDING REMARKS

In this chapter the role of a leader in creating a high-performing team was discussed. The steps in the pathway do not always follow a straight line. In reality teams move among the stages of the Tuckman Model that was discussed in Chapter 11 because:

1. **The composition of teams could change**—Established members may leave and new members may join. The team may drop down from the performing stage to the forming or storming stages. In these situations the leader's role may change from supporting or

servant leadership (removing barriers to team performance and empowering the team to self-direct) to a more direct approach. The leader would then coach the team to move up Tuckman's ladder.

2. **Circumstances could change**—Situations including natural disasters, changes in the competitive landscape, product obsolescence, corporate downsizing, takeovers, and/or new management may stress members of a team who become more focused on security, family issues, etc. These circumstances may cause performance to drop off for a period of time. In these situations, the leader can:

   • Empathize with employees concerns and practice active listening.
   • Provide tools/assistance in order to take some of the burden off of employees.
   • Modify tasks/workload in the short term to the highest priority items to help provide downtime for team members to address issues.
   • Shield employees from misinformation and gossip by communicating often, clearly, and honestly. There is no need to hide the truth; team members probably already know the truth and need to trust their leaders.

3. **Team members may not completely understand the mission**— Address situations when a team member is not aligned with the vision, mission, or goals of the team even after repeated efforts to clarify, explain, listen to concerns, etc. The leader cannot allow team members to continue to impede the performance of the team, as inaction will weaken the entire team. In such a situation the team leader can:

   • Continue to coach the team member.
   • If there is a skill problem, seek assistance from professional coaches or internal resources within the HR department if available (e.g., training).

When these attempts fail to improve the team member's performance, the leader may decide to remove the team member from the team and make an effort to find a position within the organization where the team member can fulfill their expectations or possibly help the team member find employment elsewhere.

Beyond these situations, a leader may be faced with a situation where he or she does not have the skills and/or experience required to be effective in the business or as a team leader. While it is difficult for people to accept this reality, it is far better for the leader to address it before the organization addresses the leader's lack of performance, such as:

1. Seek a coach or mentor to help develop needed skills and provide objective feedback.
2. Be open to feedback.
3. Seek a position where there is a match for their skills, experience, and style, whether that is within the current organization or in another organization.

This chapter began by asserting that great teams consistently achieve results, often exceeding expectations by applying five important steps. Let's review Jonathan's story from Section 13.5 in the context of those five steps:

1. **Trust**—The organization *trusted* the gate agent to make a decision based on the circumstances. The trust, in part, was based on training and leadership experiences within the industry since human-factor training was introduced.
2. **Commitment to mission**—The attendant was *committed to providing excellent customer service*. He considered the circumstances and decided to act in order to provide that excellent service, despite the fact it was inconvenient and somewhat uncomfortable to recover the bags in the rain.
3. **Unbridled communication**—Employees at all levels of the organization attended human-factor training. They also *shared experiences in team meetings*:
    *   What worked, what didn't work, and the related consequences.
    *   What people learned through a variety of circumstances.
    *   When it is appropriate to take action and when to escalate situations if there was a question.
    *   How to assess risks and weigh the consequences of their actions.
    *   How to assess the added value of decisions against negative potential consequences.
4. **Adapting to change**—The gate attendant was *empowered to take action* to help a customer when there was an opportunity

to change flights. There were no procedures or rules that were established to guide actions in this specific situation. The gate agent assessed the situation, took action, and created a happy customer with acceptable levels of risk.

5. **Accountability for results**—Leadership *accepts accountability* for their decision to empower employees. That accountability culture cascades down through the organization. Think about the following in the example of Jonathan's experience with the gate agent described earlier in the chapter:

   • Leadership is accountable for the safety of customers and employees.
   • The gate agent's supervisor is accountable to ensure that the members of his team are trained enough to consider factors that could negatively impact any actions they may take in providing excellent customer service.
   • The gate attendant is accountable for his actions in providing excellent customer service. The agent accomplished the mission of excellent customer service with attention to safety and the result was a satisfied customer (along with a confirmation that human-factor training was meeting its objective).

13.9 ESTABLISHING YOUR FOCUS AREAS FOR DEVELOPING A HIGH-PERFORMING TEAM

There should have been behaviors that resonated with you as you read through sections of this chapter:

- 13.1 Developing a High-Performing Team: The Role of the Leader
- 13.2 Building Trust
- 13.3 Commitment to Mission
- 13.4 Unbridled Communication
- 13.5 Adapt to Change
- 13.6 Accountability for Results
- 13.7 Leading Self-Organizing Teams
- 13.8 Concluding Remarks

List no more than three behavior-based focus areas for developing a high-performing team.

FOCUS AREAS FOR CHAPTER 13

Focus area 1—Describe a behavior-based focus area that would assist you in developing high-performing teams (e.g., ensure that employees have a clear understanding of desired outcomes):

_____

_____

_____

Focus area 2—Describe a behavior-based focus area that would assist you in developing high-performing teams:

_____

_____

_____

Focus area 3—Describe a behavior-based focus area that would assist you in developing high-performing teams:

_____

_____

_____

Don't forget to update the template you downloaded from www.jross pub.com/CLT to keep track of your focus areas created in exercises throughout this book.

13.10 SELECTING YOUR LEADERSHIP TRANSFORMATION FOCUS AREAS

In Chapter 10 you created your first draft of your behavior-based leadership focus areas and added to them in Chapters 11 through 13. Complete a final review of your focus areas and confirm that they are still valid based on the key chapter takeaways listed here:

1. **Chapter 10**—Lead To Succeed
   - What leadership is and is not
   - Leadership is about achieving results
   - Understanding why people follow
   - Listed initial behavior-based leadership focus areas, based on your experience and the leadership assessment
2. **Chapter 11**—Team Dynamics
   - Forming the team
   - The storming phase
   - Becoming a team
   - Performing as a team
   - Listed your behavior-based focus areas for improving team dynamics
3. **Chapter 12**—Coaching for Success
   - The role of leader as a coach
   - Characteristics of an effective coach
   - Coaching individuals and coaching the team
   - Tools and techniques for effective coaching
   - Listed your behavior-based focus areas for improving as a coach
4. **Chapter 13**—Good Teams to Great Teams
   - Trust
   - Commitment to mission
   - Unbridled communication
   - Accepting accountability
   - Adapting to change
   - Achieving results
   - Leading self-organizing teams
   - Listed your behavior-based focus areas for leading successful teams

Review your previous leadership focus areas and choose no more than three that you believe would have the greatest positive impact on your behaviors as a leader. Consider the following criteria when choosing your focus areas:

1. Positive impact on your work and/or personal life (high impact is preferable).

2. Time to achieve measurable results (shorter time to achieve results is preferable).
3. Difficulty in achieving results (the more difficult to achieve results, the more time and effort is required).
4. Level of your commitment (high level of personal commitment is essential).

Finally, list no more than three high-priority leadership focus areas in the space provided. As with choosing the highest-priority communication focus areas, a multi-criteria decision tool is presented in Appendix C for those readers who prefer a more rigorous methodology for selecting their high-priority focus areas.

FINAL LEADERSHIP FOCUS AREAS

Leadership high-priority focus area 1—

_____

_____

_____

Leadership high-priority focus area 2—

_____

_____

_____

Leadership high-priority focus area 3—

_____

_____

_____

Don't forget to update the template you downloaded from www.jross pub.com/CLT to keep track of your focus areas created in exercises throughout this book.

In Chapter 14 (Transformation: Develop Your Plan—Make It Happen) you will further refine your list of communication and leadership focus areas from potentially six down to the three *highest*-priority focus areas where you will develop specific goals and plans, and also identify how you will measure progress.

13.11   KEY TAKEAWAYS

1. High-performing teams do not just happen. Developing a high-performing team is an important role for leaders.
2. The pathway to developing a high-performing team starts with trust. People who follow leaders are following leaders whom they trust.
3. You have identified the behaviors of the people you trust.
4. High-performing teams are committed to the mission of the organization and how their roles contribute to that mission. High-performing teams do not avoid disagreements; rather, they know how to disagree well.
5. Leaders unbridle communication at all levels and team members share information within their team and among other teams throughout the organization. Leadership provides tools and techniques to assist with achieving unbridled communication.
6. Organizations adapt to change and support that culture throughout the organization—particularly as the organization moves into and among more complex systems. Rules, procedures, and standards are used appropriately where they create value.
7. Leaders understand the importance of developing a culture of accountability for results as the hallmark of high-performing teams. While responsibility can be assigned, accountability is accepted.
8. Leaders understand their role when working with self-organizing teams.
9. You have identified three behavior-based focus areas to increase your ability to help good teams become great teams.
10. You have selected no more than three overall high-performing leadership focus areas from the work you completed in Chapters 10–13.

ENDNOTES

1. Herzberg, Frederick. 1968. "One More Time: How Do You Motivate Employees?" *Harvard Business Review* 46, no. 1 (January–February 1968), pp. 53–62.
2. Medhi, Barasha. 2021. "5 Easy Ways to Influence Strong Organizational Commitment." Retrieved March 4, 2021, from *Vantage Circle Blog* at https://blog.vantagecircle.com/organizational-commitment/.
3. McChrystal, Stanley, Tatum Collins, David Silverman, and Chris Fussell. 2015. The story Fredrick Taylor is adapted from: *Team of Team: New Rules of Engagement for a Complex World*. New York, NY. Penguin Publishing Group. pp. 36–43.
4. Poli, Robert. 2013. "A Note on the Differences Between Complicated and Complex Social Systems." *Cadmus Journal*. 2, no. 1. Nov. 11, 2013, pp. 142–147.
5. Render, Joshua. 2019. "Distributed Teams or Collocated Team in Agile." Retrieved June 12, 2021, from *Agile-Mercurial: The Art and Science of Handling Rapid and Unpredictable Changes* at https://agile-mercurial.com/2019/02/10/distributed-teams-vs-co-located-teams-in-agile/.
6. McChrystal, Stanley, Tatum Collins, David Silverman, and Chris Fussell. 2015. The story Fredrick Taylor is adapted from: *Team of Team: New Rules of Engagement for a Complex World*. New York, NY. Penguin Publishing Group. p. 128.
7. Dagher, Kate. 2020. "What Is the Difference Between Accountability and Responsibility?" Retrieved August 3, 2021, from *Fellow* at https://fellow.app/blog/management/what-is-the-difference-between-accountability-and-responsibility/.
8. Samuel, Mark. 2006. *Creating an Accountable Organization*. Katonah, NY. Xephor Press.
9. Ibid., pp. 31–44.
10. Bossidy, Larry and Ram Charan. 2002. *Execution—The Discipline of Getting Things Done.*New York, NY. Crown Publishing. pp. 57–84.
11. Ibid.
12. Osherove, Roy. 2016. *Elastic Leadership: Growing Self Organizing Teams*, New York, NY. Simon & Schuster.

13. Surdek, Steffan. 2016. "Three Common Misunderstandings of Self-Organizing Teams." Retrieved August 14, 2021, from *Forbes* at https://www.forbes.com/sites/forbescoachescouncil/2016/12/20/three-common-misunderstandings-of-self-organized-teams/?sh=74d83fe8195e.

14. Cohn, Mike. 2017. "Two Types of Authority Leaders Must Give to Self-Organizing Teams." Retrieved July 21, 2021, from Mountain Goat Software at https://www.mountaingoatsoftware.com/blog/two-types-of-authority-leaders-must-give-to-self-organizing-teams.

15. Nicolette, Dave. 2018. "Limits of Self-Organizing Teams." Retrieved July 2021, from https://www.leadingagile.com/2018/06/limits-of-a-self-organizing-team/.

16. "Agile Self-Organizing Teams: What They Are and Why They Work." Retrieved from Lucidspark at https://lucidspark.com/blog/agile-self-organizing-teams.

Part III

Transformation

CHAPTER 14

TRANSFORMATION: DEVELOP YOUR PLAN—MAKE IT HAPPEN

"Some people want it to happen, some wish it would happen; others make it happen."

—Michael Jordan

CHAPTER ROADMAP

You have reached the capstone chapter in this book—the *make it happen* chapter where you will complete a final prioritization of behaviors that underpin your personal transformation and/or your team's transformation to a high-performing team. As you work through this chapter, make a decision whether your personal transformation is an essential enabler of your team's transformation. If that is the case, Section 14.1 will help you focus initially on your own personal transformation. Section 14.2, *Transforming Your Team*, lays out a leadership transformation plan to help you define the aspiration for your team, including plans and measures to develop a commitment for your team members in order to transform a good team into a great one. As with other chapters, it concludes with a summary of key takeaways.

14.1 YOUR PERSONAL TRANSFORMATIONAL JOURNEY

The exercises in Chapters 9, *Presenting Is Leading*, and 13, *Good Teams to Great Teams*, resulted in a list of your high-priority focus areas for *communication* and *leadership*. It is now time to prioritize those focus areas from six down to no more than three of the *highest*-priority focus areas. Why three? We have previously stated that your commitment to changing your behaviors will depend on whether or not you achieve your goals. In the absence of meaningful results, our experiences inform us that other personal and work priorities will overwhelm your motivation to change important behaviors. Consequently, we recommend limiting your focus areas. While it is your decision as to how many focus areas you choose, we raise a red flag if you choose more than five. In addition, consider that you will be creating goals, plans to achieve those goals, and metrics to measure progress toward your goals.

To begin the prioritization process, gather your high-priority focus areas for communication and leadership. Score them on the criteria listed here:

1. Positive impact on your work and/or personal life (high impact is preferable).
2. Time to achieve measurable results (shorter time to achieve results is preferable).
3. Difficulty in achieving results (the more difficult to achieve results, the more time and effort is required).
4. Level of your commitment (high level of personal commitment is essential).

You can also use the multi-criteria decision tool in Appendix C to prioritize focus areas if you prefer a more rigorous approach.

As you complete these exercises, list no more than three of your highest-priority focus areas:

FINAL FOCUS AREAS FOR IMPROVEMENT

Highest priority focus area 1—(e.g., when asked for my opinion or recommendation, be more decisive and direct with my answer):

_____

_____

_____

Highest priority focus area 2—

_____

_____

_____

Highest priority focus area 3—

_____

_____

_____

Don't forget to update the template you downloaded from www.jrosspub .com/CLT to keep track of your focus areas created in exercises throughout this book.

From this list of your highest-priority focus areas, establish goals, plans to achieve those goals, metrics to measure progress toward your goals, and sources of feedback (sources of feedback may already be in your metrics, and if so, there is no need to complete the sources of feedback section). If the focus area itself is a goal, don't overthink it. List the focus area as the goal. Nevertheless, a goal should be SMART:

> **S—Specific:** Clear on what the goal means
> **M—Measurable:** Define the evidence to show you are making progress
> **A—Attainable:** A stretch but reasonably attainable
> **R—Relevant:** Consistent with the focus area
> **T—Time-bound:** A realistic end date to achieve the goal

The following format is a narrative approach. For readers who prefer a more rigorous approach with tables to assist in being more specific, see Appendix D for a more formal template. We have also included a filled-out example on the following pages:

1. **List focus area:**
   When asked for my opinion or recommendation, be more decisive and direct with my answer.

- **Goal:**

  Improve efficiencies and streamline processes by removing uncertainty from directives.

- **Plans to achieve the goal:**

  Solicit feedback from peers and family, asking if my answer is clear and decisive.

  If I am not ready to give an answer, let people know and set a deadline for the answer or recommendation.

  Keep a log of when I am told I am decisive/direct or indecisive/indirect.

  Self-assess on goal achievement at the end of each week.

- **Performance metric (how you will measure progress):**

  General trend of increasing decisiveness/directness in log

  Record how often I proactively ask for feedback on responses

- **Sources of feedback, type of feedback requested (e.g., coaching and/or evaluation):**

  Seek feedback from peers, managers, and direct reports who can observe me in situations where I respond to questions. Establish a baseline with those who I ask for support.

1. **List focus area:**

   _____

   _____

   _____

- **Goal:**

   _____

   _____

   _____

- Plans to achieve the goal:

  _____

  _____

  _____

- Performance metric (how you will measure progress):

  _____

  _____

  _____

- Sources of feedback, type of feedback requested (e.g., coaching and/or evaluation):

  _____

  _____

  _____

2. List focus area:

   _____

   _____

   _____

   - Goal:

     _____

     _____

     _____

- **Plans to achieve the goal:**

  _____

  _____

  _____

- **Performance metric (how you will measure progress):**

  _____

  _____

  _____

- **Sources of feedback, type of feedback requested (e.g., coaching and/or evaluation):**

  _____

  _____

  _____

3. **List focus area:**

   _____

   _____

   _____

   - **Goal:**

     _____

     _____

     _____

- **Plans to achieve the goal:**

  _____

  _____

  _____

- **Performance metric (how you will measure progress):**

  _____

  _____

  _____

- **Sources of feedback, type of feedback requested (e.g., coaching and/or evaluation):**

  _____

  _____

  _____

Congratulations, you have successfully completed:

1. Assessing and selecting behavior-based goals where you have committed to improve.
2. A plan that outlines how you will practice the behaviors that support the skill areas that are important to you in your work and personal life.
3. Defining how you will measure that you are moving toward your goals to improve your communication and/or leadership behaviors.
4. Sources of feedback to *coach* you along your journey.

As you achieve your goals, you can add additional ones for improvement. Remember, transformation is a journey, not a destination.

14.2   TRANSFORMING YOUR TEAM

Communication and leadership skills underpin the ability of a leader to assist his or her team's journey to the high-performance space. Members of high-performing teams are committed to the vision and work of the team. When leaders communicate, they understand that they are not talking to employees or to an audience; in their minds, they are talking to constituents. And constituents get to vote (and that vote can be silent but exhibited by behavior) as to whether they will follow, comply, or commit. The following eight-step method shows how leaders can communicate to build a high-performing team:

1. **Find the connection**—Great leaders must understand the needs of their constituents. This was discussed in Section 6.3, *Going Forward: Creating a Relationship Building Strategy*. Questions that constituents ask may include:
   - Does this leader know where he or she is heading? Is it clear to his/her constituents.
   - Does this leader really believe what he or she is saying? Great leaders believe in themselves; they believe in the mission and the goals. In that belief, they are honest about potential trials, tribulations, and setbacks (e.g., the leader is invested personally in the mission for which she/he is requesting a commitment, rather than quoting public relations jargon).
   - Is this leader connecting with the needs and interests of their constituents? Recall that people who follow leaders are looking for trust, compassion, stability, and hope. One of the best ways to connect with constituents is a personal story that connects with the needs of constituents and is a basis for the aspiration.
2. **The vision**—This cannot be a marketing statement, but the leader's *personal commitment* to a vision of the future (e.g., the aspiration). It is a stretch, there are risks, and there are implications for those impacted. The leader must have a realistic plan to achieve the aspiration.
3. **The plan**—The leader offers a plan, in broad terms, on how the team can achieve the vision. The plan outlines the critical success factors, one of which is the team's commitment. It also outlines key milestones, risks, and how progress will be measured. This plan cascades down through the organization so that efforts are

aligned with the aspiration and it gains more detail on *how* the aspiration will be achieved.

4. **Implications for those involved**—The leader informs people about how achieving the vision of the future will impact them (i.e., the constituents). It is paramount that the leader is honest and open about the implications for those involved in:
   - Shutting down a division
   - Changing a job
   - Moving to a new location
   - Learning new skills

5. **Why now?**—Explain why it is necessary to achieve the vision now. Many people may be comfortable with the status quo (e.g., no need for change), or they are distrustful of leaders who talk a good game yet fall short on providing what teams need to be successful. They want stability today, but they also want hope for the future. As a leader, spell out the consequences of not moving now.

6. **Specific requests**—The leader provides specific examples of what he or she is asking people to do, such as:
   - Learn new jobs
   - Move their family
   - Support the effort of coworkers, vendors, etc.

7. **Benefits**—The leader explains the benefits for those involved in achieving the aspiration and must answer the key question: What's in it for the constituents?

8. **The tough issues**—Address the *hardball* issues. List and anticipate the questions that you hope no one will ask. Then, answer the questions before someone asks them. If tough issues are not addressed, constituents are left to conclude one, or both, of the following (neither of which are good):
   - The leader doesn't know the major concerns or issues
   - The leader knows the concerns but doesn't care or doesn't have an answer

Develop your leadership message by following the guidelines presented in Chapter 9, *Presenting Is Leading*; using your lessons learned from other chapters; and remembering your experiences and observations.

While moving your team into the high-performance space, there are some key points to remember from previous chapters:

1. Hire the right people and assure they are in the right job. The *A* players are not always the smartest. The *A* players are those who are *committed* to the vision, strategies, and work of the organization.
2. Be accurate in your praise and coaching for improvement rather than being charitable or kind. While people may prefer positive feedback, *accurate* feedback is more helpful.
3. Do not allow loyalty to trump what is best for the organization. Be able to make the difficult decisions regarding who is on the team.
4. Fail fast and allow the team to learn from mistakes. Do not let people make mistakes that have unacceptable consequences. Your team needs a governance structure that assures that the right people are involved in high-risk decisions.

A valid question is, "What does a leader do when people have clear direction, the skills and resources needed to perform their jobs, the time needed to achieve results, and yet commitments and results are not achieved?" In this case, it may be necessary to move people to a position where they can be successful, or coach them off the team.

Congratulations on completing the work outlined in this book. We know the exercises involved effort and, as we have mentioned throughout this book, change is hard. That is to say, hard work to climb out of the wheel ruts that may be keeping you in less productive habits of communication and leadership. We encourage you to continue working toward improving these behaviors. Let the journey begin!

14.3 KEY TAKEAWAYS

1. You have identified your highest-priority behavior-based focus areas for improvement based on the work done in Part I: *Communication* and Part II: *Leadership.*
2. You have transformed your highest-priority focus areas into goals, plans to achieve those goals, how you will measure progress, and sources of feedback.
3. You have developed a leadership message to lead your team to the status of a high-performing team.
4. You have completed the work necessary for achieving success as a communicator and a leader.

THE JOHARI WINDOW

In Chapter 3 we discussed the importance of understanding our personality traits since it influences how we send and receive communications. In that chapter the INSIGHT Inventory® was offered as a tool to provide feedback on our personality profile. Besides completing the INSIGHT Inventory® ourselves, the tool can be used to have others provide us feedback on how they perceive our personality traits. Another tool to obtain information about how we see ourselves and how others see us is the *Johari Window*. In this tool, a participant selects adjectives from an established list that they believe describes themselves. Others select adjectives from that same list that they believe describes the participant. The selections are then arranged in a four-quadrant window, as shown here:

Johari Window

	Known by self	Unknown by self
Known by others	Adjectives selected by participant and others	Adjectives selected only by others (blind spots)
Unknown by others	Adjectives selected only by the participant	Adjectives selected by neither participant nor others

After the window is completed, the participant and the others who have provided feedback discuss the results, and then the information is shared. This exercise is not complex, can be instructive, and may help uncover blind spots. It can be accessed at this URL: https://kevan .org/johari.

An example of how a team can use the Johari exercise is provided at this link: https://www.seerinteractive.com/blog/the-johari-window-a -simple-exercise-to-improve-your-one-on-one-meetings/.

RELATIONSHIP-BUILDING TOOL

Note: Visit www.jrosspub.com/CLT to download a blank version of this template.

Person	Needs they have that you can help with	Needs you have that they can help with	Connecting activities	When/timing		
				Weekly	Monthly	Quarterly
Name, Person #1	1.	1.	1.			
	2.	2.	2.			
	3.	3.	3.			
Name, Person #2	1.	1.	1.			
	2.	2.	2.			
	3.	3.	3.			

MULTI-CRITERIA DECISION TOOL

The purpose of this tool is to help you prioritize your behavior-based focus areas according to how they rank on specific selection criteria. The selection criteria used in the tool below are:

1. Positive impact on work or personal life (weight 0.3). High score is desirable.
2. Time required to achieve measurable results (weight 0.2). A high score means less time.
3. Difficulty in achieving results (weight 0.2). A high score means low difficulty.
4. Level of personal commitment (weight 0.3). A high score is desirable.

These criteria and their weights are listed in the column headings in the following example table. To use the tool, list your focus areas in the first column. In the rows for each focus area, apply a score from 1 to 5 for each criterion where:

- A score of 1 means no impact/most time/most difficulty/no commitment
- A score of 2 means little impact/more time/more difficulty/little commitment
- A score of 3 means some impact/some time/some difficulty/some commitment
- A score of 4 means high impact/little time/little difficulty/high commitment
- A score of 5 means highest impact/least time/least difficulty/highest commitment

Communication Goal/ Focus Area	Positive impact on work and/or personal life Weight = 0.3	Time required to achieve measurable results in three months Weight = 0.2	Difficulty of achieving results Weight = 0.2	Level of personal commitment Weight = 0.3	Total score equals the sum of weight times score for the four criteria
#1: Listen to people in order to understand, not just to respond	Score = 3 Weighted score = 0.9 (0.3 × 3)	Score = 5 Weighted score = 1 (0.2 × 5)	Score = 3 Weighted score = 0.6 (0.2 × 3)	Score = 3 Weighted score = 0.9 (0.3 × 3)	Total weighted score = 3.4 (0.9 + 1 + 0.6 + 0.9)
#2 Before giving feedback, ask the person to self-assess and build on their assessment to support and offer suggestions for improvement	Score = 4 Weighted score = 1.2	Score = 3 Weighted score = 0.6	Score = 3 Weighted score = 0.6	Score = 3 Weighted score = 0.9	Total weighted score = 3.3
#3 Build relationships, e.g., connections with people whose support I will need to achieve desired results	Score = 5 Weighted score = 1.5	Score = 3 Weighted score = 0.6	Score = 2 Weighted score = 0.4	Score = 4 Weighted score = 1.2	Total weighted score = 3.7

The table on the next page is an example of three hypothetical communication focus areas.

Referring to the table on the previous page, the first focus area listed is: "Listen to people in order to understand, not just to respond." The score applied across the rows for the criteria are listed here:

1. Positive impact on work or personal life. Score is 3—some impact.
2. Time required to achieve measurable results. Score is 5—least time required.
3. Difficulty in achieving results. Score is 3—some (or average) difficulty.
4. Level of personal commitment. Score is 4—high commitment.

Multiply each score by its corresponding weight and enter the total score in the last column. The total scores for each of the three communication focus areas in the example is shown here:

- Focus area 1 total score: 3.4
- Focus area 2 total score: 3.3
- Focus area 3 total score: 3.7

In this example, focus area 3 would be the highest priority, followed by focus area 1, with focus area 2 being the lowest priority.

The table on the next page is provided for you to list and score your focus areas to determine the order of priority.

Leadership Goal/Focus Area	Positive impact on work and/or personal life Weight = 0.3	Time required to achieve measurable results in 3 months Weight = 0.2	Difficulty of achieving results Weight = 0.2	Level of personal commitment Weight = 0.3	Total score equals the sum of weight times score for the four criteria
#1	Score =	Score =	Score =	Score =	Total score =
#2	Score =	Score =	Score =	Score =	Total score =
#3	Score =	Score =	Score =	Score =	Total score =
#4	Score =	Score =	Score =	Score =	Total score =
#5	Score =	Score =	Score =	Score =	Total score =

Note: Visit www.jrosspub.com/CLT to download an excel spreadsheet template with built-in formulas that will calculate your totals.

GOALS, PLANNING, AND METRICS TEMPLATES

Note: Visit www.jrosspub.com/CLT to download a blank version of this template that you can complete.

LIST FOCUS AREA 1: _____

_____

_____

From this focus area, list a behavior-based goal or goals. If the focus area itself is a goal, don't overthink it. List the focus area as the goal. The goal should be SMART.

> **S**—Specific: The goal is absolutely clear
> **M**—Measurable: Define the metrics that show progress
> **A**—Attainable: It can be a stretch, but should be reasonably attainable
> **R**—Relevant: Consistent with the focus area
> **T**—Time-bound: A realistic end date to achieve the goal

Goal 1

State the Goal: _____

_____

_____

Goal measure	Yes	No
Is it specific/clear?		
Is it measurable?		
Is it attainable?		
Is it relevant?		
Is it time-bound?		

If any answer is no, then rewrite the goal until all answers are yes.

Plan: List the activities you will complete to reach your goal.

	Date to complete	Resources needed	Help from others
Activity 1 (describe)			
Activity 2 (describe)			
Activity 3 (describe)			

Metrics: Describe how progress will be measured (e.g., feedback from others, your own satisfaction with specific criteria such as quality of presentation, listening without interrupting, articulating a vision, etc.)

	Very poor/ Not at all satisfied	Poor/ Slightly satisfied	Fair/ Moderately satisfied	Good/ Very satisfied	Excellent/ Completely satisfied
Three to five key points					

Sources of feedback, type of feedback requested (e.g., coaching and/or evaluation):

_____

_____

_____

LIST FOCUS AREA 2: _____

_____

_____

From this focus area, list a behavior-based goal or goals. If the focus area itself is a goal, don't overthink it. List the focus area as the goal. The goal should be SMART.

Goal 2

State the Goal: _____

_____

_____

Goal measure	Yes	No
Is it specific/clear?		
Is it measurable?		
Is it attainable?		
Is it relevant?		
Is it time-bound?		

If any answer is no, then rewrite the goal until all answers are yes.

Plan: List the activities you will complete to reach your goal.

	Date to complete	Resources needed	Help from others
Activity 1 (describe)			
Activity 2 (describe)			
Activity 3 (describe)			

Metrics: Describe how progress will be measured (e.g., feedback from others, your own satisfaction with specific criteria such as quality of presentation, listening without interrupting, articulating a vision)

	Very poor/ Not at all satisfied	Poor/ Slightly satisfied	Fair/ Moderately satisfied	Good/ Very satisfied	Excellent/ Completely satisfied
Three to five key points					

Sources of feedback, type of feedback requested (e.g., coaching and/or evaluation):

_____

_____

_____

LIST FOCUS AREA 3: _____

_____

_____

From this focus area, list a behavior-based goal or goals. If the focus area itself is a goal, don't overthink it. List the focus area as the goal. The goal should be SMART.

Goal 3

State the Goal: _____

_____

_____

Goal measure	Yes	No
Is it specific/clear?		
Is it measurable?		
Is it attainable?		
Is it relevant?		
Is it time-bound?		

If any answer is no, then rewrite the goal until all answers are yes.

Plan: List the activities you will complete to reach your goal.

	Date to complete	Resources needed	Help from others
Activity 1 (describe)			
Activity 2 (describe)			
Activity 3 (describe)			

Metrics: Describe how progress will be measured (e.g., feedback from others, your own satisfaction with specific criteria such as quality of presentation, listening without interrupting, articulating a vision, etc.)

	Very poor/ Not at all satisfied	Poor/ Slightly satisfied	Fair/ Moderately satisfied	Good/ Very satisfied	Excellent/ Completely satisfied
Three to five key points					

Sources of feedback, type of feedback requested (e.g., coaching and/or evaluation):

_____

_____

_____

EXAMPLE: TEAM GROUND RULES

1. Help us stay on schedule; use the one-to-five decision tool to keep us moving without limiting time on important matters.
2. Participate actively.
3. Listen to each other. Provide timely recognition and constructive feedback to each other.
4. Avoid speeches when making your points.
5. Make your thinking visible.
6. Provide clear, honest, and candid comments and opinions during discussions and decisions.
7. Visibly support *team* decisions through words and actions.
8. Be on time.
9. Plan to stay until the end—it will end on time.
10. Follow good meeting etiquette—no cell phones, etc.
11. Do not take team business outside of the team without permission.
12. Address issues/concerns you have with a team member's behavior directly with that team member.
13. We will all participate in *one conversation*; there will be no side conversations.

FACILITATION GUIDE

You may be called upon to facilitate a group for any number of reasons. Consider this an opportunity for impromptu leadership. This guide will provide tips and techniques for facilitating a group.

WHY FACILITATION SKILLS MATTER

When you facilitate a group, you are expected to lead the group to a conclusion, a resolution, or specific results. The ability to facilitate effectively reflects on you as a leader, whether or not you are the leader of the group being facilitated. Having the right mindset and experience contributes to an effective facilitation. Your challenge as a facilitator is that you need to obtain consensus among individuals with different personalities, mindsets, perspectives, and experience. Typically, the situations that require facilitation call for a resolution or conclusions within a very short period of time—anywhere from a couple of hours to a couple of days. Sometimes the time frame may be longer, but that time frame will be composed of a series of sessions. Although the time frame may be short, the results of the facilitation can have long-term impacts.

Situations that may call for short-term facilitation include, but are not limited to, the following:

1. Vision setting for a project
2. Defining a mission for an organization or team
3. Problem solving and root cause analysis
4. Producing project documents (charter, scope, schedule, etc.)
5. Risk assessment
6. Emergency situations
7. Tactical plans
8. Strategic direction

SUCCESS FACTORS FOR EFFECTIVE FACILITATION

The following list explains some of the key success factors for effective facilitation:

1. **Pre-session preparation**—Be clear about the purpose of the session. Know the location and, if possible, scout the location ahead of time to better understand any constraints and prevent any last-minute surprises. You should know the number of participants and also know as much as possible about each participant that is relevant to the session. Identify any potential barriers to success and determine how you would deal with them. Understand any scheduling and time constraints. Also, prepare a timed agenda and communicate that agenda ahead of time.

2. **Process**—Have a process to guide you through the facilitation. Understand and be able to articulate to the group how you will arrive at your destination (the goal or objective of the session). One of your primary roles is to own the process and to use the process to draw the results from the participants. As the facilitator, you should not be influencing the results or introducing any bias.

3. **Plan the opening**—The opening is important because it sets the tone for the entire session. Determine how you will kick off the session and handle the presentation of the objectives. Consider how you will introduce the agenda or roadmap for the session and how to handle the introductions of the participants. If each participant will be introducing him or herself, provide some guidance for the introduction that includes the time allowed. You might consider having each participant define what he or she might consider a successful outcome.

4. **Use ground rules**—Establish ground rules or guidelines to be used by all participants and obtain agreement or *buy-in* from each participant. Have the ground rules posted visibly as a reminder to all. The following list contains some ground rule examples:
   - Time is to be respected
   - Do not stray from the agenda (unless all agree to modify)
   - Treat everyone as equals (no titles)
   - Everyone contributes
   - Listen respectfully to each person's input
   - Suspend personal agendas

- Be open to new ideas and approaches
- Remember that there are no dumb ideas
- Remember that there are no dumb questions
- Do not allow interruptions when someone has the *floor*
- Do not allow side conversations

5. **Use parking lots**—Use a *parking lot* to post items, questions, or issues that are not immediately relevant to the agenda. You can acknowledge those items but be quick to note that they will be posted to a list (parking lot) and not addressed as part of the agenda. Items that are posted to the parking lot may or may not be addressed outside of the facilitated session.

6. **Ensure engagement**—Be observant and ensure that all participants are engaged. Ask questions of all. If you see anyone become disengaged, explore or just ask for his/her thoughts. If appropriate, you might consider breaking up the participants into smaller groups with each group having a specific objective.

7. **Value all contributions**—Value everyone's contributions even though the contribution may not be popular or may conflict with your personal opinion. Use those opportunities to explore and probe; understand the *why* for the contribution.

8. **Manage time**—Make it clear up front that time will be respected and use ground rules to help enforce it. Always end at the promised closing time. If it is clear that more time is required, obtain consensus for a follow-up meeting, but do not consider extending the session unless you had communicated up front that the session might be extended.

9. **Seek closure**—Always keep the focus on the goals or objectives of the session and work to seek closure. Set aside some time on the agenda for obtaining consensus or closure.

10. **Encourage collaborative techniques**—Promote collaboration by using voting processes, posting ideas on the wall or whiteboard, and having all participants engage in the decision-making process.

INDEX